Critical Guides to German Texts

12. Weiss: Marat/Sade

Critical Guides to German Texts

EDITED BY MARTIN SWALES

WEISS

Die Verfolgung und Ermordung Jean Paul Marats dargestellt durch die Schauspielgruppe des Hospizes zu Charenton unter Anleitung des Herrn de Sade

Ian Hilton

Senior Lecturer
University of Wales, Bangor

Grant & Cutler Ltd
1990

© Grant & Cutler Ltd 1990

ISBN 0 7293 0320 9

I.S.B.N. 84-599-3069-6

DEPÓSITO LEGAL: V. 1.702 - 1990

Printed in Spain by
Artes Gráficas Soler, S.A., Valencia
for
GRANT & CUTLER LTD
55-57 GREAT MARLBOROUGH STREET, LONDON, W1V 2AY

Contents

Contents

Prefatory Note

Quotations from *Marat/Sade* take as their source the fifth version of the play revised by the author and to be found in the Edition Suhrkamp edition, published by Suhrkamp Verlag, Frankfurt am Main, 1965. Other references, indicated in brackets by an italicized number, are to the numbered items listed in the Select Bibliography, followed by the page number.

In keeping with the intention of the series in general, this present contribution seeks to provide an introductory and essentially informative study of what was, and has remained, one of the outstanding achievements in the post-1945 German theatre.

My debt of gratitude is owed to Mr Ludvík Kundera for his unfailing encouragement.

Prologue

Dieser Dramatiker hat eines der
großen Theaterstücke unseres
Jahrhunderts geschrieben.
(Hans Mayer, *Rede auf Peter Weiss*)

Not surprisingly, the bicentenary year of the French Revolution is currently marked by the publication of new studies of the age as well as the reissue of contemporary views and verdicts, and, not least, the reappearance of diverse writings of major figures of the day. These include works of Jean Paul Marat. The Akademie Verlag of East Berlin, for example, is in the process of publishing German translations of his very important *Philosophical Essay on Man* (1773), originally published in English whilst Marat was exiled in Britain, and of the early political work, *The Chains of Slavery* (1774), an attack on despotism addressed to British voters in which he expounds — arguably for the first time — the notion of an 'aristocratic' or 'court' plot. The latter work had already appeared in 1988 in a new French edition, *Les Chaînes de l'Eslavage* (Complexe, Paris). Both of these writings by Marat are referred to in Peter Weiss's play *Marat/Sade*.

From this side of the Channel, the events of those years in France have tended to become synonymous with all the horrors that took place, the reign of terror, the wars that followed Bonaparte's seizure of power, rather than with the possible bliss of being a participant at the dawn of a new political direction to life. On German soil, Goethe would doubtless have been of similar mind. Of Goethe's attitude to the 'Morgenröte einer kommenden Zeit' Peter Weiss writes: 'Goethe gewährt der *revolutionären* Auseinandersetzung keinen Raum, stellt aber ausführlich die *Evolution* der Klassenbeziehung dar', and again: 'G abgestoßen von

der revolutionären Macht der franz. Volksmassen' (*8*, p.31). Goethe's
stance was of course not one shared by all across the Rhine.
Certainly Wieland, Herder, Fichte, Schelling, Hegel, Jean Paul,
Kant, Schiller and Hölderlin, for example, were in favour, at least in
the early stages, of what Klopstock described, in his ode 'Kennet
euch selbst', written in August 1789, as 'Des Jahrhunderts edelste
Tat'.

German literature has frequently made thematic use of the
French Revolution, many works concentrating in fact on its leading
figures. Büchner's *Dantons Tod* (1837) is but one — albeit arguably
the best known — example in this connection from the nineteenth
century. In our day Peter Weiss has added his contribution. The
Encyclopaedia Britannica, in its entry on Jean Paul Marat, includes
the following comment: 'His name became much more familiar in
the Western world through the popularity of the play by Peter
Weiss.' The play in question is *Marat/Sade* (1964).

Weiss's words on Goethe in the *Notizbuch*, quoted above, were
written at the time when he was occupied with the reworking of his
later play *Hölderlin*, which had first been performed in 1971. Interest
in the historical figures from both banks of the Rhine, Marat and
Hölderlin, provided the inspiration and the working basis for Weiss
to complete two major plays that bear witness to the weight of the
Revolution in his own consciousness.

1. The Place of Marat/Sade in the Context of Post-1945 German Drama and of Peter Weiss's Career

'Total theatre with no holds barred...' (*34*), '...seit Brechts Tod das erste bedeutendere Bühnenwerk eines Deutschen...' (*16*, p.58) are just two of the typical tags liberally attached by critics to Peter Weiss's *Marat/Sade* in their reviews of the play, first performed in 1964. The generally lavish praise bestowed upon the piece was to be seen not only as recognition of its own real merits but also as reflecting in part new hopes for the German theatre overall, hopes that seemed to be coming to fruition in the course of the sixties. German theatre had recovered only slowly after the Second World War. Having been denied, or having themselves denied, foreign drama for several years, German theatre-going audiences and dramatists alike after 1945 understandably wished to receive once more the external stimuli so long missing. Initially, the works of Eliot and Fry, Wilder and O'Neill, of Claudel, Sartre and Anouilh, and of Lorca supplemented the fare of the native classics: the plays of Lessing, Kleist, Goethe and Schiller. Among contemporary German-speaking playwrights, it was initially the 'outsiders' who found public fame: Carl Zuckmayer, already an established literary name, had crossed the Atlantic after the advent of Nazism, but returned after the war (thus bridging the gap, as it were, between past and present) and achieved a stunning success with his play *Des Teufels General*, first performed in 1946 in Zürich; or they were geographical 'outsiders' like the Austrian Fritz Hochwälder and the Swiss writers Max Frisch and Friedrich Dürrenmatt. Indeed for well over a decade the Swiss, it has been popularly accepted, seemed almost alone to carry the flag for contemporary German drama with a string of plays before they were joined in the van in the early sixties by new talent. It was a talent that was immediately recognized internationally and whose work, with its focus on recent history, gave rise, under the guidance of the director Ernst Piscator, famed already from earlier years, to so-called 'documentary theatre'. Rolf Hochhuth set the pace in 1963 with *Der Stellvertreter*, closely followed by Heinar Kipphardt (*In der Sache J. Robert Oppenheimer*, 1964) and Peter Weiss, whose play *Die Ermittlung* (1965) was staged the year after his first major dramatic success, namely *Marat/Sade*.

Peter Weiss's first ever published work (in the Swedish language) had appeared soon after the end of the war; the third volume of his novel *Die Ästhetik des Widerstands* was in the bookshops the year before his death in 1982. His published writings therefore span thirty-five years and *Marat/Sade* occurs at a pivotal stage in that period, not merely in the sense that it was written at roughly a mid-point in his literary career, but, more important, that it served to mark the close of that phase of his work which had produced 'experimental', 'surrealistic', 'pantomimic', 'grotesque', 'shadowy' (the epithets are ones regularly applied by the critics to Weiss's early writings) works in both prose narrative (*Der Schatten des Körpers des Kutschers*, 1960; *Das Gespräch der drei Gehenden*, 1963) and in dramatic form (*Der Turm*, 1948; *Die Versicherung*, 1952; *Nacht mit Gästen*, 1963; *Wie dem Herrn Mockinpott das Leiden ausgetrieben wird*, begun 1963). At the same time, *Marat/Sade* also shows the way forward to the next phase of historical, more political pieces for the theatre over the next decade: *Die Ermittlung* (1965), *Gesang vom Lusitanischen Popanz* (1967), *Vietnam Diskurs* (1968), *Trotzki im Exil* (1970), *Hölderlin* (1971), *Der Prozeß* (1975) and his prose *tour de force* of the seventies, *Die Ästhetik des Widerstands*. All of these writings are stamped with his Marxist beliefs and faith in socialism as a panacea for the world's ills.

Weiss traces his painful journey of self-discovery as artist and *zoon politikon* in various prose writings. The narratives *Abschied von den Eltern* (1961) and *Fluchtpunkt* (1962), whose very titles point to restless wanderings, record a spiritual autobiography up to the age of thirty. Both that early and the post-war periods find further sporadic coverage in the *Notizbücher 1960-1971* (1982) and *Notizbücher 1971-1980* (1981). The entries provide telling, private glimpses into his hopes and fears, his literary aspirations, political dilemmas, human concerns. Last but by no menas least in this process of self-revelation is the three-volume 'anti-fascist historical novel' *Die Ästhetik des Widerstands*, which represents Weiss's extended attempt to work out, in his own words, 'eine kämpfende Ästhetik'.

He was born on 8 November 1916 in Nowawes (now Babelsberg) near Berlin. His father Eugen Weiss was a prosperous textile manufacturer and a Czech Jew who had fought in the Austro-Hungarian army in the First World War; his mother was Frieda Hummel, a Swiss Lutheran and formerly an actress. The early years were spent primarily in Bremen, where the family had moved at the end of the war. An interest in, and a talent for, painting was noted early on, for after the family moved back to Berlin in 1929, he took art classes under Eugen Spiro at the Kunstgewerbeschule in Berlin in 1932. With Hitler's rise to power in 1933, the family chose to emigrate the following year. His father's political sympathies undoubtedly helped to determine that course of action ('mein Vater äußerte Verständnis für Trotzki...' (*8*, p.120). The first period of exile was spent in England (Chislehurst and London), where Peter Weiss studied photography at the London Polytechnic. Two years later the family returned to the continent to live in the Bohemian town of Warnsdorf, where the father worked in the Samtweberei Frölich. Peter studied at the Academy of Art in Prague under Willi Nowak. The two years spent in Czechoslovakia were the worst years of his life. They were, as he was to recall, years without hope: 'war vor allem Defätist, wollte mich nicht anwerben lassen zur Armee, in England, in der Tschechoslovakei. Meine Interessen Literatur, Kunst — ' (*8*, p.44). This same profound pessimism — 'Die defätistische Frage, warum überhaupt schreiben, Kunst, angesichts des bevorstehenden Todes, des gesamten Untergangs' (*8*, p.115) — colours his creative drive. His paintings accordingly emphasized *angst*-ridden apocalyptic visions, a world of dark fantasy. One of his paintings, entitled 'Sturmmaschinen', he described in a letter to Hermann Hesse of December 1937 as 'eine Art neuer Romantik aber

um Gottes Willen nicht im archaistischen Sinne und nicht im Sinne
von Mondschwärmerei — nur der Wille, von der schrecklichen
Mechanisierung und Verflachung loszukommen' (*11*, p.24). To be
sure, many of his paintings in the thirties reveal aspects of isolation
and loneliness; there is little sense of open space. Rather do we see
scenes where people are enclosed as in a prison yard. One picture
from the Prague days, painted in 1937, is in fact entitled 'Im Hof des
Irrenhauses'. And of another from the same time, 'Gartenkonzert'
(1938), Weiss writes: '[Meine Schwester] sah mich zwischen den
Konzertierenden im Garten am Cembalo sitzen, mit entstellten
Gesichtsausdruck, als Insasse eines Irrenhauses' (*5*, p.28). The way
ahead seems indeed to point to *Marat/Sade*! The more so perhaps
when we read a comment on Weiss's painting 'Theaterszene' (1935):
'eine intuitivere Vorwegnahme der Choreographie der Ideen und
Leidenschaften in 'Marat/Sade', als führte hier nicht der Marquis,
sondern die Corday selbst die Regie' (*33*, p.9).

Once more the life of wandering beckoned and by the summer
of 1938 he was in Switzerland again (having gone the previous
summer to Montagnola). The visit was a success for Weiss: he was
employed by Hermann Hesse to illustrate one or two of the latter's
stories. Hesse ('eine Figur in meiner psychologischen Landschaft',
33, p.15) proved an early spiritual mentor and wrote favourably of
his protegé to Kubin in the autumn of that year. But in fact Weiss's
stay in Switzerland was tolerated for only a few months by the
authorities who arrested him as a suspect alien. By the end of
September German troops had already occupied Bohemia and
Moravia. In the spring of 1939 in fact, Weiss was deprived of his
Czech nationality, but allowed into Sweden on an alien's pass
because he had the security of his parents to fall back on (they
themselves had moved from Czechoslovakia to Sweden in 1938, see
5, p.14). Peter Weiss's story is that of a typical representative of the
first half of the twentieth century: the stranded Central European,
driven about by crises, persecutions, wars, a product of the inter-war
years, whose rootlessness can be seen as part of the historical
process.

Sweden was to remain Weiss's chosen home for the rest of his life, initially in Alingsås from the spring to the autumn of 1939, and then in Stockholm. He found employment in forestry work for a time, and at his father's works learned, in his desire for total assimilation, the Swedish language (as assiduously as he had English in the two years he was in England), associated with members of the banned German Communist Party, mixed with Swedish writers and artists. Indeed his first words in print appeared in Swedish soon after the end of the Second World War — two modest collections of prose poems. His first play *Der Turm* (1948) was also written originally in Swedish, as was *Das Duell*. Exhibitions of his paintings were also held: in 1941 in Stockholm, in 1946 in Gothenburg. In 1945 he acquired Swedish nationality. In 1964 he married Gunilla Palmstierna, a ceramics artist and designer, who was to work closely with her husband on the staging of his plays. To his death he remained a member of the Swedish Communist Party.

In one very real sense, however, the testing time still lay ahead for Weiss with the termination of the Second World War. How was he, an emigrant, to reacquaint himself with Germany — and the German language? 'Die Abwehr gegen Rückkehr nach Deutschland — die Sprachlaute die mit den Jahren vor der Emigration verbunden waren. — Zusammenzucken bei Hören. Das Unheimliche im Zug auf der Reise nach Hamburg' (*8*, p.640). The occasion was the summer of 1947; the purpose of his visit to Germany, to write articles for a Stockholm daily newspaper on the current cultural situation:

> Die Artikel, die sich mit der kulturellen Situation im geschlagnen Deutschland befaßten, schrieb ich auf schwedisch...Die deutsche Sprache war mir fremd geworden. Ich dachte u träumte auf schwedisch. Das Deutsch, das ich jetzt hörte, übersetzte ich ins Schwedisch...Als Ausländer, als Schwede kam ich zurück in ein Land, aus dem ich einmal vertrieben worden war. Es verband mich nichts mehr mit diesem Land. Auch der Haß, den ich einmal empfunden hatte,

der mich die Sprache, die ich in der Kindheit erlernt
hatte, verleugnen ließ, war verschwunden. Doch die
Verwüstung, die mich umgab, erinnerte stetig an die
unselige Politik des Faschismus. Die Menschen waren
gezeichnet von einer gänzlich fehlgeschlagnen
Geschichte...Im Sommer 47, in den Trümmern Berlins,
begann ich, nach neuen Zusammenhängen zu suchen.

Es fing an mit der Sprache. (*8*, pp.678f.)

It was to prove a long, painful struggle:

1947 — alles was seitdem geschah, ist Folge dieses
grundlegenden Betrugs an den Erwartungen einer
Erneuerung — Da ich zu objektiv sicheren Resultaten
doch nicht kommen konnte, schienen mir die
Mechanismen des Traums am besten den Reaktionen auf
die heutigen Zustände zu entsprechen. (*8*, pp.673f.)

Such an approach seemed to many an inappropriate response to life
at that time. In 1947, for example, Peter Suhrkamp was to write
apropos a manuscript which Weiss had submitted, entitled *Der
Vogelfreie*, that its visions remained fantasies of an inner world, their
reality not the reality of other people[1]. 'Hier zeigte es sich am
deutlichsten, wie weit wir uns auseinandergelebt hatten', Weiss later
commented (*8*, p.675).

The struggle to come to terms with the contemporary reality of
Germany was still fraught with difficulties for Weiss. From 1952 he
had sent the manuscripts of *Der Schatten des Körpers des Kutschers*
and *Die Versicherung* to numerous German publishing houses —
with a signal lack of positive response. In the interim he felt that he
had progressed to his limits with his paintings (exhibitions of his
work continued nevertheless to be shown at various galleries over
the next thirty years — in, for example, West and East Berlin,

---

[1]*Briefe an die Autoren*, 1963, Bibliothek Suhrkamp, 100, pp.55-58.

Bremen, Bochum, Munich, Södertälje, Zürich, Paris, Rostock, Stockholm — and reveal Weiss to be a painter of talent widely recognized in the international world of art). For him, painting had become now too immobile ('ein statisches Medium'), too limited; he felt his pictures were merely 'Ausschnitte, Fenster, Blicke in mein Guckkastentheater' (5, p.65). Being dissatisfied with the expression of a single moment, he turned to moving pictures, and there followed in the fifties a phase of film-making. There were short experimental films - Weiss called them 'Studies' — like *Waking up* (1952) and *Hallucinations* (1955), each of six minutes duration. The latter 'führt ein fast abstraktes Ballett aus Armen, Beinen und Körpern vor. Die verzweifelten Versuche, etwas zu fassen, zu essen oder zu trinken, scheitern. Die Kamera bleibt auf Bruchstücke der Handlungen fixiert' (*11*, p.26). It was a time when Weiss was avidly taken with the theory and practice of surrealist art and film, an interest which finds written expression in 'Avantgarde Film', an essay he wrote in the early fifties, though it was not published in Germany until a decade later.[2] He also made a few documentary films that suggest his concern with social problems of the underprivileged, the outsider: *Faces in Shadow* (1956) examines the daily impoverished routine of some 'down-and-outs' in the old part of the city of Stockholm. *In the Name of the Law* (1957) depicts the routine existence of young offenders in a reform institution. With the camera concentrating on objects — barred windows, closed doors — Weiss captures the sense of isolation, the frustration and rebellion of these youths (*11*, p.33). The following year he was again tackling a social problem of youth — alcoholism, in *What do we do now?* (1958). The same year saw the making too of a full-length feature film, *The Mirage*, 'a poem of a day in the city, a complex film about finding a way to exist' (*36*). Films provided Weiss with but temporary respite from his dilemma. His essential concern was with writing. But his work on canvas and celluloid can be — should be — regarded as foreshadowing his writings, not least those for the theatre. His career as painter and cineaste shows Weiss adopting two approaches: the one allowed for creating surrealistic collage, a seemingly random

---

[2]*Akzente*, 10 Jhg, 1963, 307ff.

association product of a fertile imagination; the other focused on a more objective, documentary presentation of life with a concrete social comment to impart. This interplay of modes is further in evidence in his writings, wherein too the strong visual effects of art and the cinema provide a particular force and vividness. This is as true of the prose narrative *Der Schatten des Körpers des Kutschers* as of his plays *Die Versicherung, Trotzki im Exil*. We shall encounter it also in *Marat/Sade*. As Weiss himself commented: 'Bildkunst, Schreiben und Film bleiben bei mir die Einheit einer totalen Kunst, in der man sich nur jeweils verschiedner Instrumente bedient.' (*16*, p.15).

The turning point for Weiss as a writer came with the publishing of *Der Schatten des Körpers des Kutschers* by Suhrkamp. The year was 1960, Weiss then 43. Not that all doubts were resolved: 'Doch von welcher Art ist dieser Einstieg in die deutsche Literatur gewesen, gehörte ich überhaupt der deutschen Literatur an, blieb ich nicht bis heute ein Außenseiter?' (*8*, p.727). The sense of being an outsider was to haunt Weiss throughout his life. Whilst Sweden remained nominally his home, he found the country politically sleepy. On the other hand, he could not stay in Germany, though he did try to settle in West Berlin on more than one occasion. From the early sixties there was, however, a fundamental change in Weiss's political attitudes. Up to the late forties, Kafka's world, which Weiss associated with defeatism (*5*, pp.164ff.), had dominated the latter's heart and mind. Then the reading of Henry Miller's *Tropic of Cancer*, with its images of sexual rebellion, had proved a startlingly powerful release for Weiss. The mood of pessimism that had clouded his earlier years inexorably receded before an advancing tide of radicalism. For Weiss, this was initially an aesthetic radicalism that reflected his interest in surrealism, but from the early sixties the emphasis fell more on a political radicalism. Rebellion against authority, the call for 'Redefreiheit' and 'offene Kritik', the desire for more active involvement in the social, political and cultural issues of the times, found expression in his writings from *Marat/Sade* onwards, particularly so as he came to regard uncommitted artistic expression to be more of a condoning of fascism than a release from bourgeois beliefs and values. And Weiss's change of attitude came at a time in the sixties when Germans in general were beginning to cast a more critical eye at the world and at politics — a state of affairs stimulated by such events as the Eichmann trial in Jerusalem and the Auschwitz trials in Frankfurt which superseded the earlier *Vergangenheitsbewältigung* syndrome in people's minds. The identification of art and politics was spelt out with the utmost clarity by Weiss in *Zehn Arbeitspunkte eines Autors in einer geteilten Welt*; these first were announced in the Stockholm paper *Dagens Nyheter* of 1 September 1965, but quickly reprinted in both the Federal Republic (*Theater Heute*) and the Democratic Republic (*Neues Deutschland*). The message was unambiguous: 'Zwischen den beiden Wahlmöglichkeiten, die mir heute bleiben, sehe ich nur in der sozialistischen Gesellschaftsordnung die Möglichkeit zur Beseitigung der bestehenden Mißverhältnisse in der Welt' (*14*, p.118). It was a polemical, political attitude on Weiss's part that won him as many enemies as friends. The *Notizbuch* entry for 30 March 1972 records:

> Grass (unter andern): weil sie meine politische Einstellung ablehnen, lehnen sie auch meine literarischen Arbeiten ab. Ihre spöttischen Bemerkungen zu meiner polit. Haltung betreffen ebenso meine Bücher. Politik u Schreiben ist für mich eins. Für sie auch, aber bei ihnen die Politik liberal, reformistisch. Immer wieder: eine uralte parteipol. Gegnerschaft, übertragen aufs Kulturelle —. (*8*, pp.56f.)

And we similarly note an embittered comment in the entry for 25th June of the following year:

> Wieder ist es ihnen geglückt, mich beim Büchnerpreis zu umgehn. Diesmal ist er an Handke vergeben worden. Nun haben die meisten von denen, die von mir gelernt haben, den Preis bekommen, und mir wird er, aus eindeutig politischen Gründen, vorenthalten. Hätte ihn

etwa 1965 bekommen sollen, doch da hatte ich gerade
meine 10 Arbeitspunkte publiziert. (*8*, p.221)

(In fact he was to be awarded it in the year of his death.)

Illustrations of Weiss's commitment and his involvement in
controversy abound. As one example, we think of 'Unter dem
Hirseberg', his contribution to Hans Werner Richter's collection of
essays and viewpoints in support of the Social Democrats during the
Federal election campaign of 1965, *Plädoyer für eine neue
Regierung oder Keine Alternative* (Rowohlt: Reinbek bei Hamburg,
1965). (By 1969 Weiss was no longer ready to support the SPD any
further.) At the Gruppe 47 meeting at Princeton University in 1966,
Weiss, against the advice of Richter, chose to speak out to the
students at a protest meeting against the Vietnam war. That same
year he took issue with Hans Magnus Enzensberger on the latter's
discussion of what he saw as the real divide in world politics. ('Eine
Kontroverse', *Kursbuch* 6, 1966, pp.170ff.). In 1967 he visited Cuba,
his resultant piece *Che Guevara!* appearing the following year. His
support for Vietnam remained constant. In February of 1968 he had
added his signature to the 'Erklärung zur Internationalen Konferenz'
in West Berlin. That summer he served on the Lord Russell Tribunal
and visited North Vietnam for five and a half weeks. Whilst not
taking up arms in defence of that country (as Enzensberger had
urged Weiss and fellow sympathizers to do), Weiss continued to
give undiminished written support to Vietnam to the end of his life.[3]
Turning to the Middle East, he spoke out on the Israeli War; on the
European front — in the spirit of open criticism and free discussion
— he wrote letters to the Czech Writers Union, the Bulgarian
Writers Union, to the Russian *Literaturnaia Gazeta*, the Czech paper
Rudé Pravo, *Die Zeit*, the *Frankfurter Allgemeine Zeitung*, *inter alia*
on a variety of issues ranging from the Biermann affair to the
occupation of Czechoslovakia following the Prague Spring, to the
Helsinki Agreement.

---

[3] e.g. 'In Sachen Humanität. Zur Lage in Vietnam', in *Frankfurter Rundschau*
29.11.1978; 'Noch ein Vietnam', in *Kultur und Gesellschaft* 3 (1979), Heft
10, 3-6.

A certain frustration with life in Sweden, a positive dissatisfaction with it in West Germany did not make things any easier for Weiss elsewhere. His stated declaration of alignment with the tenets of belief espoused in East Germany failed, for example, to evoke the degree of enthusiasm there which Weiss may have hoped to elicit. It is true that in both Germanies (as elsewhere) *Marat/Sade*, *Die Ermittlung, Abschied von den Eltern* had attained undoubted success and popular approval in the mid-sixties. Acclaim for his later work came more grudgingly. He could, for instance, find no West German theatre initially prepared to stage his dramatization in revue form of colonial persecutions in Angola and hence took *Gesang vom Lusitanischen Popanz* to Stockholm for its première. Even there controversy surrounded both play and author, also at the London production two years later. The piece was first performed on 26 January 1967 at the Scala Theatre. On 4th February the Portuguese Foreign Office decried the play as irresponsible and complained to Sweden for allowing it to be produced. As a result of the subsequent London performance at the Aldwych Theatre on 6 May 1969 by the Negro Ensemble Company of New York as part of the World Theatre Season, the Attorney General asked the Director of Public Prosecutions to look into an M.P.'s demand for investigation with a view to the prosecution of Mr Weiss for incitement to racial hatred against the white people of Great Britain. Though no further action in fact was taken, the provocation of Weiss's theatre in performance certainly attracted front-page attention in the national daily press at the time. (Shades of the British reaction, though for different reasons, to Rolf Hochhuth's play *Soldaten* in England!). Equally, his *Vietnam Diskurs* certainly did not meet with American approval. On the other hand, *Trotzki im Exil* aroused the profoundest criticism in the Soviet Union and East Germany. The crushing of the Czech search for a 'socialism with a human face' in 1968, which Weiss saw as detrimental to the global struggle for socialism, provided the stimulus for his contribution to the Lenin Year: 'I have made it my business to remind socialists (among whom I count myself) of what happened in their history' (*Times*, 21 June 1969). The socialists of the Soviet Union and East Germany were not happy nor indeed prepared to be reminded in this fashion of the questionable historical past of their nation and spoke of ideological sabotage ('Mit meinem Stück über Trotzki hatte ich ein Tabu verletzt', (*8*, p.691). For two years Weiss remained a *persona non grata* in the eyes of the authorities in the German Democratic Republic. Indeed Marcel Reich-Ranicki was convinced that Weiss never really recovered from the disappointment occasioned by this 'Trotzki-Komplex', and that all of his late work should be viewed in that context (*Frankfurter Allgemeine Zeitung*, 12 May 1982). How shaken Weiss was by this experience and how he felt himself to be in a political vacuum, may be gauged from the five-page entry in the *Notizbuch* for 24 November 1971 (*8*, pp.24-28) which tells of an arranged meeting in East Berlin with Hager and Abusch to discuss, on the one hand, the possible staging of *Hölderlin* in East Germany that Weiss hoped for, and on the other, the question of a disavowal by Weiss of his play *Trotzki im Exil*, something that the East German authorities keenly desired. In the event, *Hölderlin* was eventually staged; the matter of *Trotzki im Exil* was left on the table. The actual attendance of Abusch and Hager at the eventual Rostock première of *Hölderlin* on 16 June 1973 (the production was by Hanns Anselm Perten, who had been responsible for the earlier East German première of *Marat/Sade* in 1965) at last signified official acceptance once more.

Hölderlin was rated a box-office success in West German theatres, though Weiss again was not in full agreement with every production (*8*, p.13) and indeed felt that the Stuttgart version of the former East German director Peter Palitzsch was the only one to come close to his expectations. Weiss's next theatrical venture took him back once more to the familiar world of Kafka, to a dramatic adaptation of *Der Prozeß* which was premièred in Bremen in 1975. But Kafka's distorted perspective on the world in his novel gives way now, in Weiss's hands, to a more objective and historically concrete presentation, with the setting of the play in a potentially revolutionary situation in the old Austro-Hungarian Empire before the outbreak of the First World War. The West German critics were not impressed, as Weiss remarks:

> Im Theater, in der Pause, ging Rischbieter mit dem
> Gesichtsausdruck an mir vorbei, der besagte: das
> Todesurteil über dich ist gefallen!
> Auch Karaseks Rezension im Spiegel war eine
> Hinrichtung. Sehr kurz. Durch Nackenschuß. (*8*, p.429)

A revised version of the piece was, however, successfully performed
in 1977 at the Volkstheater in Rostock!

Around this time too Weiss's collected plays were published
(*9*), but in fact for the last decade of his life he was preoccupied once
more with narrative prose, undertaking his most ambitious project,
the three-volumed 'Wunschautobiographie' *Die Ästhetik des
Widerstands* (1974, 1978, 1981). A thousand pages long, set in Nazi
Germany, Spain at the time of the Civil War, in Sweden at the time
of the Second World War, and with a narrator this time from a
proletarian background, the novel sets out to examine the social role
of the arts, a subject that had of course filled Weiss's thoughts
throughout his own artistic career. The problematic issues in the
novel were not, however, satisfactorily resolved — at least for
literary critics of both right and left political persuasions. Weiss's
exasperated reaction to one such critic is recorded in an entry to the
Notizbuch:

> Auch er hat garnicht kapiert, daß er einen Roman liest,
> auch nichts verstanden vom Wesen der Ich-Figur, in der
> sich alle zur Sprache gebrachten Gegensätze u
> Meinungsverschiedenheiten brechen. (*8*, p.810)

To his chagrin, Weiss could not envisage the early publication in
East Germany of this work and expressed his concern accordingly
(*8*, pp.758-60). The reader gains, incidentally, important insights into
Die Ästhetik des Widerstands through the *Notizbücher 1971-1980*
which were published simultaneously with the third and final
volume of the novel (The *Notizbücher 1960-1971*, again in two
volumes, appeared in 1982).

Weiss had directed his own play *Der neue Prozeß* in Stockholm shortly before his death in May 1982, following ill health. But *Die Ästhetik des Widerstands*, a major achievement by any standards, serves as a better epitaph.

2. Genesis

The first reference by Weiss to Marat in the *Notizbücher 1960-71* (7, p.111) is to be found in an entry for 17 February 1963. Some thirty pages later, at the start of the section covering the period 20.4.-4.10.1963, we can read Weiss's summary of how the germ of an idea gave birth to a play that was to enjoy international acclaim:

erste Gedanken zu MARAT im Nov. 62, blätterte mit Gs [Gunilla Palmstiernas] Sohn Micke in dem Standardwerk DIE FRANZÖSISCHE REVOLUTION, stieß auf das Bild Marats in der Badewanne — hatte in der eigenen Schulzeit schon von dem Revolutionär in der Wanne gehört. Plan entstand zu einem Hörspiel: die Ermordung Marats. Konfrontation zunächst nur Marat-Corday. Revolution-Konterrevolution. Erst im Februar 63, als ich in der Galerie Springer die Vorbereitungen für meine Ausstellung im November traf, nahm der Plan Gestalt an. Die Dramatik Marat-Corday war zu einfach gewesen, suchte nach einem stärkeren Gegenspieler, nach reicheren Verknüpfungen. Gespräche mit Alexander Kowal waren inspirierend. Wir kamen auf Sade zu sprechen, dessen Werke ich seit Mitte der 50er Jahre kannte, in der engl. Übersetzung der Olympia Press. Als Gegensatz zu Marat Sade geeignet, doch wie ließen sie sich miteinander verbinden? Kowal erinnerte daran, daß Sade die Rede bei Marats Begräbnis gehalten hatte. Er, der Individualist - hält die Gedenkrede auf den Kollektivisten? Aber was gab es sonst für Beziehungen? Ich wollte nichts erfinden, sondern von historischem Sachverhalt ausgehn. Bei weiteren Gesprächen mit

Kowal: Sade hatte während seiner Internierung in
Charenton Theatervorstellungen abgehalten! Las darüber
nach in der Sade-Bibliographie von Lely. Plötzlich war
die dramatische Struktur gegeben. Das Stück konnte
abrollen —

In a pen-portrait of Peter Weiss, entitled 'Marats Trommel',
Hans Werner Richter provides another perspective (*37*). The latter
recalls an occasion one night in the early sixties (he does not specify
the date) when he and Peter Weiss met in a bar in Berlin. It was after
midnight when Weiss began to talk of his literary plans. He wanted
to write a piece for the the theatre, was still uncertain, however,
about the theme, other than that it should deal with a historical
figure, a controversial figure who should nevertheless accord with
his own political viewpoint. To this end he had already been thinking
of Marat, in his view the really great tragic figure of the French
Revolution. Other suggestions offered by Richter and the barman
'Karlchen' — Robespierre, Fouché, Richelieu, Henry IV — were
aired, and rejected. For his part, Richter was not convinced of the
suitability of Marat for a modern play. Discussion on Marat and the
French Revolution raged on for hours. 'Three or four months later'
(again, Richter is not precise, other than saying that it was already
spring; it would, however, definitely have had to be before the end of
the third week of April), Richter heard the daily staccato clacking of
a typewriter along a corridor in the Berlin Academy of Arts. Weiss
was absorbed in bringing Marat to life.

The thirty or so pages in the *Notizbuch* referred to above
provide fascinating glimpses of how the project took shape: the
mention of discussions with Kowal, the titles of reading material on
Marat by Gottschalk and Rosbroj for his own research purposes, the
jotting down of ideas, fragments of dialogue, motivation, stage
setting — all this gathers momentum, acquires fluency, takes shape
on the page before our eyes. The two-finger typewriting lasted from
1st March to 20th April. An entry in the *Notizbuch* for 21st April
reads: 'Reinschrift MARAT beendet.' In the *Materialienbuch* (*14*,
pp.29-57) that appeared in 1967 as an informatory companion piece

to the play itself, Weiss spells out the precise nature of the variations in the five versions of *Marat/Sade* he was to produce between 1963 and 1965. Suffice to say here that the versions reflect the playwright's hesitant journey of political belief from West Berlin to Rostock; from an open-ended, ambivalent standpoint to an expression of Marxist commitment still tinged with his lingering doubts and uncertainties. The major changes in terms of content affect the Epilogue; the scenic presentation undergoes frequent change — for practical, theatrical reasons, for example, to highlight the importance of the debate between Marat and Sade, to determine more clearly the role of the audience on stage and its relationship with the audience off stage. The first two versions were hectographed for stage productions; the third, fourth and fifth appeared in book form.

The first version, completed in April 1963, comprised a prologue and two acts with no further subdivisions. There were few scenic directions provided. The final scene contained a restatement of their respective arguments and positions adopted in the course of the play by Sade, Marat, Corday and Roux. Almost immediately Weiss started work on a second version, entailing this time the division of the play into three acts and the addition of stage directions. The content of the play remained basically the same, save that Sade's own final argument in the last scene was now omitted. This second version was completed by June of that same year. The following month Weiss met with the young Polish director Konrad Swinarski to discuss the staging of the play; not long after that he conferred with Hans-Martin Majewski about the necessary music.

In the autumn of 1963 the meeting of the Gruppe 47 was held at the Kleber-Post in Saulgau. Peter Weiss, together with Gunilla Palmstierna, attended from Stockholm. He wanted to read from his *Marat* text, but insisted on performing the Song of the Vendée to the accompaniment of beats from a drum which he held between his legs and played. (A drum had been found for him somewhere in Saulgau.) It proved an evening to remember, as Richter recounts (*37*):

Alle waren überrascht, der überlange Titel erregte
Verwunderung, einige lachten zuerst, doch die Unruhe
legte sich schnell. Peter ließ sich nicht stören, er las und
trommelte eine Dreiviertelstunde lang, scheinbar die
Ruhe selbst. Ich spürte Ablehnung im Saal, ich sah es an
diesem oder jenem Gesicht, und nur wenig Zustimmung.
Die Knittelverse kamen nicht recht an, manche hielten
sie wohl für völlig unliterarisch, nur geeignet für
Sonntagsreden und Hochzeitsgedichte, auch der
Rhythmus der Trommel konnte da nicht viel helfen...Als
Peter geendet hatte und die Trommel neben sich stellte,
sah ich zum Teil mißvergnügte, zum Teil ratlose
Gesichter. Ein Gespräch kam nur langsam in Gang,
kritische Äußerungen gab es genug, aber auch verhaltene
vorsichtige Zustimmung. Was dem einen positiv
vorkam, erschien dem anderen negativ. Einige waren
neugierig auf das Ganze, sie versprachen sich zwar kein
Theaterstück davon, aber doch ein Schauspiel in Versen,
das wahrscheinlich niemals eine Bühne beleben würde.
Trotzdem hatte Peters Auftritt etwas Sensationelles an
sich.

The uniqueness of the occasion described by Richter above is
confirmed by Marcel Reich-Ranicki: 'Unvergeßlich ist für alle, die
daran teilgenommen hatten, jener Abend im Herbst 1963' (*FAZ*, 12
May 1982). Weiss recalled the reaction too and later commented in
the *Notizbuch*:

Böse sah es Grass. Er äußerte diesmal nur, daß ich
schlecht getrommelt hätte.
Hans Mayer war es, der mich, mit plötzlichem Ein-
springen, aus schon gewichtig werdenden Angriffen
errettete. (*8*, p.731)

Notwithstanding the mixed reactions he encountered in
Saulgau - perhaps spurred on by them — Weiss got down

straightaway in November to revising the *Marat* material still further. He had not in any case been satisfied with the second version. Now in the third version the play was divided into just two acts, with thirty-three scenes. Again, there was not much change in the text as such, apart from the last scene where the final arguments, of Marat, Corday and Roux (as well as of Sade) are now omitted. Stage directions became more detailed, also some variations in the style of the piece occurred, whereby contrasting combinations were now to be better emphasized, the *Knittelvers* (which Richter for one had not thought to be an appropriate form) rubbing shoulders with the literary style of Sade and Marat, the 'sing-song' of Charlotte Corday. Weiss acknowledged the valuable advice given him in the reworking of the material — particularly relating to Scenes 1, 27 and 33 — by Swinarski, who was in fact to direct the play now scheduled for production in the April of 1964 at the Schiller Theater in West Berlin. According to the *Notizbuch* (7, pp.198-200), the reworking commenced on 19th November and was completed on 7th December (though Peter Weiss's 'Nachbemerkung zu "Marat/Sade"' actually states 'Weiterarbeit November 1963 - März 1964' (p.144). Three months of rehearsal ensued before the première took place on 29 April 1964. Four months later, on 20th August, Peter Brook's production of the play (translated by Geoffrey Skelton with verse adaptation by Adrian Mitchell) was performed for the first time at the Aldwych Theatre in London, again after three months of rehearsal. By the autumn of that year Weiss was hard at work on the fourth version of his play, this time concentrating on changes in the text itself that accorded with his ever evolving political belief in Marxism and with an eye to the staging of *Marat/Sade* in East Germany. The significant addition in this respect was the insertion in the Epilogue, amidst the tumult of the patients, of Roux's call 'When will you learn to see'. Hanns Anselm Perten (who was to collaborate further with Weiss over the years) took two months to rehearse the version performed on the stage of the Volkstheater in Rostock for the first time on 26 March 1965. The Czech première of *Marat/Sade*, translated by Ludvík Kundera, took place in Brno in May of that year under the direction of Evžen Sokolovsky following three

months of rehearsals. Already in the preceeding month — so the
entry in the *Notizbuch* for 18 April 1965 informs us — Weiss had
completed yet another, the fifth, version of Marat for a new
Suhrkamp edition. The major change in content here again concerns
the Epilogue. Roux's outcry at the end which had been introduced in
the fourth version remained, but also restored again after their
omission in the third and fourth versions were the speeches of Sade,
Marat, Corday and Roux that restate their earlier positions. Sạde's
sceptical statement now occupies a prominent final position and the
play ends in an open question. This fifth version — coming so
relatively soon after the version prepared for the Rostock staging —
might be interpreted as a significant retrogression in Weiss's political
belief. On the one hand, he is on record as affirming:

> Von meiner sozialistischer Stellungnahme her habe ich
> Marat nicht nur als die geschichtliche Figur aus einer
> betrogenen Revolution zeichnen wollen, sondern als
> einen Visionär, von dem aus die Linie zu künftigen
> Revolutionen läuft. (*14*, p.112)

On the other, in virtually the same breath, he claims that his
adherence to an uncommitted 'third' position stems from his political
ignorance at the time. In short, the versions show Weiss to be
walking a politico-theatrical tightrope and we shall return later to
this point (see Chapter 7).

Weiss's play was quickly translated in fact into a dozen
languages and published in book form in the period 1965-1966 in
Britain, the United States, Mexico, Japan, Russia, Hungary, Poland,
Czechoslovakia, Finland, Sweden, Norway, Denmark, France, The
Netherlands, Italy, as well as appearing in both West and East
Germany (*14*, pp.161-63). Similarly, productions of the play were
mounted in Cologne, Essen, Wiesbaden, Braunschweig, Hamburg,
Düsseldorf, Heidelberg, Freiburg, Vienna, Lyons, Paris, Milan,
Stockholm, Warsaw, New York...the list of theatres staging the play
lengthened, testimony to the international popular appeal of Weiss's
work. The dramatic impact then was world wide. But in fact the

West Berlin, Rostock and London productions were generally held to be the major yet highly different stagings that set the tone and the standard for future and numerous interpretations of *Marat/Sade*.

Weiss, Peter, 1916— und her Jur pruilt notes, worversenathiy heid
in se the effect of stilb hyllize soppmiig ihment the mun. 20 fune
domenof Achrus and ninrious deganicourations th theovonw

3. Time, Place, Plot

Immediately eye-catching and thought-provoking is the very length of the play's title: *Die Verfolgung und Ermordung Jean Paul Marats dargestellt durch die Schauspielgruppe des Hospizes zu Charenton unter Anleitung des Herrn de Sade*. The mention of Marat and De Sade indicates that the play claims to have some historical basis. Indeed Weiss is at pains to authenticate his subject-matter by providing five pages of 'Anmerkungen zum geschichtlichen Hintergrund unseres Stückes' (1963) which form an appendix to the play (pp.139-43) and had been included too in the *Materialien zu Peter Weiss' 'Marat/Sade'* (1967). A form of historical drama, relying as it does on recorded public events, is created — a historical collage indeed, tracing the rise and fall of France's revolutionary fervour. Corday's murder of Marat as he was drafting a 'Call to the people of France' is authenticated fact. And Weiss extensively incorporates in his play authentic speeches made by Marat. Such items point to the documentary theatre, though *Marat/Sade* does not belong in the company of documentary plays as exemplified by such of Weiss's later plays as *Die Ermittlung* or *Vietnam Diskurs*. The primary invention in Weiss's play is the meeting of Marat and Sade (though, historically Sade did deliver Marat's funeral oration). Their meeting might seem at first sight to be in the mould of classic confrontations of historical drama: Danton and Robespierre in Büchner's *Dantons Tod*, Elizabeth and Mary in Schiller's *Maria Stuart*, Egmont and Orange in Goethe's *Egmont*. But Weiss did not intend Marat and Sade to be persuasive historical *characters* as such. (Indeed, the playwright is at pains to make clear that all the characters, be they the patients, Coulmier or Sade, are play-acting). Marat and Sade serve rather as mouthpieces for the presenting of contrasting viewpoints on the French Revolution, though their exchanges remain inconclusive — neither convinces the other, no position gets modified. In fact, the rationality of their social and political debate is eventually smothered by the show of anarchy by the patients/actors in the surrealistic, volatile, theatrical context. And to this end 'a hundred and one spectacular tricks are pulled out of the theatrical rag-bag' (*34*). Such 'tricks' include multiple levels of statements, patterns of opposites, the creation of illusions to be matched by the deliberate stripping away of such stage illusion. They are all 'tricks' ultimately designed by Weiss to show that 'the whole is a theatrical statement not historical reconstruction, which emphasizes that there is "a lesson", a consequence to be drawn from the action.'[4] It does permit Weiss, however, to write his dramatic essay on the reasons why the French Revolution — and, by extension, all subsequent revolutions — devoured its own children and produced a regime that created a reign of terror. The play, therefore, has a direct social and political relevance, for 'the playwright's concern was not with his characters' "insanity", but with the psychopathology of society for which the asylum setting was used as a metaphor.'[5] As he declared in an interview, Weiss saw the modern world as 'mad and far too complicated to be understood' (*36*). Weiss sets his play in the mental hospital precisely to mirror the merging of political and psychological action. No wonder then, as we shall see, that Weiss alludes on occasion in his play to situations known to contemporary audiences, such as the experiences of Nazi death camps. (As a reference point, incidentally, we might recall Friederich Dürrenmatt's own intention to make an effective social and political point with his comedy *Die Physiker* (1962), set in a mental hospital; of similar relevance would be a narrative work considered important for its criticism of the age, namely Ferdinand Gustav Kühne's *Eine Quarantäne im Irrenhause* (1835), where the narrator is interned, because of radical agitation, in a mental hospital (the setting is in reality the asylum of Sonnenstein in Saxony.)

---

[4]C. Innes, *Modern German Drama*, Cambridge University Press, 1979, p.160.
[5]Hanne Castein, 'German Social Drama in the 1960s', in *Themes in Drama*, Vol. 1, Cambridge University Press, 1979, p.195.

The title of Weiss's play also begins to point to the complexity of the piece, hints at its formalized interweaving of time and place and action. The synopsis of the play is succinctly put: 'Against a seething and crucially interruptive human backcloth of insanity, De Sade and Marat debate their contrasting philosophies of absolute individualism and unswerving dedication to social revolution, while the historical events leading up to Marat's assassination are acted out.'[6] For what Weiss presents before his off-stage audience is a play within a play, where the inmates of the mental asylum at Charenton under the direction of the Marquis de Sade mount a re-enactment of Jean Paul Marat's assassination at the hands of Charlotte Corday. This action historically occurred in Paris when Corday came to Marat's door three times on Saturday, 13 July 1793 and murdered him in his bath. The re-enactment is 'performed' on the 13 July 1808, fifteen years exactly after Marat's actual death. The setting for this 'outer' play is the asylum at Charenton (a well-known mental hospital outside Paris, which Victor Hugo's brother Eugene later entered in 1822). There the Marquis de Sade was interned from 1801 to his death in 1814 on the orders of Napoleon, who was offended ostensibly by the personalities in his pamphlet *Zoloë et ses acolytes*. During the years of his confinement at Charenton — and we know that this is fact — Sade did put on, with the permission and encouragement of the director of the asylum, plays from time to time for the therapeutic benefit of the patients. The audience for the 'inner' play produced by Sade on this fictitious occasion is in fact provided by Coulmier, the director at Charenton, and his family. They sit to one side of the stage on a raised dais and act as a kind of framework to the whole. Yet as an audience, they too have an affinity with the audience off stage, and in consequence there emerges a third level of statement on the time scale — that is, the present day of us as contemporary play-goers. It is an involvement emphasized, as we shall see, by characters on stage directly addressing the off-stage audience from time to time.

Equally vital — and as complex — is the spatial factor. The single setting for the play is the communal bath-house in the asylum.

---

[6]*Theatre Quarterly*, No.1, 1971, 44.

On the one hand, it has to serve, as far as the inner play is concerned, as a back-drop for the historical events of 1793 (and with reference back to 1789); the demise of the *ancien régime*, the meeting of the National Assembly, the reign of terror in the streets with the beheading of victims by the guillotine, the action of Charlotte Corday arriving in Paris from Caen, the assassination of Marat in his bath. The bath-house also serves as the scene of Marat's imaginary visions made physically present on stage. Marat's bath itself fulfils multiple functions: not only is it a source of respite for Marat from the sufferings from his psychosomatic skin disease, it becomes the 'podium' for his debate with Sade, the tribune for his speech to the National Assembly; ultimately it is his deathbed and coffin. In all that sense the bath (and bath-house) represents a closed world of episodes from the historical past and stressed as such by the very fact that they occur in the inner play. On the other hand, those very events are extended beyond that time-space confinement to the post-revolutionary time of the Napoleonic Empire and the year 1808. This enters therefore the second time-space dimension, but even here — and already working through from the first 'inner' level — a third level is introduced to suggest a contemporary relevance through the demarcation of limiting historical time and space factors, in that the on-stage audience merges with that off stage and involves the latter accordingly in an active sense as participants, in, as well as spectators of, the events enacted on stage.

Marat/Sade comprises two acts, some 130 pages of text in the fifth version, in the Edition Suhrkamp edition of 1965. There is no formal link between the two acts save the numerical division of scenes (Act I, Scenes 1-26; Act II, Scenes 27-33). The scenes themselves are not necessarily continuous thematically or chronologically, nor are they all determinable as far as time and place are concerned (see, for example, Scenes 14, 26). And not all involve speech or indeed action, as the opening scenes of the play immediately make clear. Scene 1 comprises just directions relating to the stage setting and merely involves the 'actors' taking their places on stage, whilst Scene 3 allows the actors briefly to prepare themselves for the performance and amounts to half a dozen lines of stage direction. By the same token, Scene 2 has no action, merely the first spoken words: twenty-eight lines of introduction delivered by the Director of Charenton, Coulmier. Not until Scene 5, therefore, does the inner play actually get under way and action begin. The thematic climax of this inner play is the assassination of Marat. But Weiss, skilfully employing the historical fact that Corday came to Marat's door three times on that fateful day, has her make her first entry in Scene 7 and the first visit in Scene 9. It is, however, a brief appearance, as Sade reminds the inmate playing the role of Corday that she has to come to the door three times. In short, the audience is made aware early on in the play of Corday's intent; the outcome is known and there is no real progression as such in the action. Her second visit does not occur until Scene 25, again of brief duration. Scene 29 is preparation for Corday's third visit; Scene 30 the actual visit. In Scene 32 the murder is committed. The Herald's words 'Der Mord', by way of announcement, are the only ones spoken in the scene. The act as such has been delayed — and deliberately so by Sade/Weiss — through the insertion of the musical history that constitutes Scene 31. The fact that the deed is perpetrated in the penultimate scene — Scene 33 is the Epilogue — permits in one sense a suitable dramatic climax to the inner play, but equally it is clear that the murder is essentially no more than a secondary issue in Weiss's thinking. Weiss signally fails to concentrate in real depth on the event itself, merely suggesting the build-up of possible tension in that we know the murder will occur only at the third and last visit. The centre of the perspective is provided by the debate between Marat and Sade, so the horizons of time and place in that context are deliberately ignored — rather, broken — by Weiss to make room for the theoretical discussion between the two. And here Weiss allows himself latitude in the matter of historicity. For the encounter between Sade, known primarily for his licentious behaviour and writings, and Marat, a leading radical of the French Revolution, is one completely invented by Weiss for his own dramatic and philosophic purposes. As earlier indicated, the relationship of Sade and Marat rests historically on the fact that the former spoke the memorial address at the Pantheon. There is a certain irony in the situation, for Sade, though being freed from the Bastille by the Revolution and then espousing its cause with some zeal for a period, arguably felt himself obliged to deliver the oration at the particular time as a matter of expediency brought about by the very political precariousness of his own position and therefore had to praise the achievements of a man whose policies he came to oppose. But it is in fact this very difference of views that Weiss now takes up with such imaginativeness to form the central feature of his own play, a dialectic that the shortened and popularly recognized version of the play's title, *Marat/Sade*, cogently highlights.

4. Marat and Sade

We have noted how Weiss's schoolboy awareness of Marat ('Schon während der Schulzeit war dieser Marat für mich ein Held', *19*, p.681) was eventually, many years later, transformed into the resolve to write a piece based on that historical figure. In turning to Marat, Weiss believed he was finding a life situation that paralleled his own perceived position of inner, and outer, exile. Born in May 1743, Marat spent his early years in obscurity in France and abroad, before becoming a well-known doctor in London (and partly in Edinburgh). He published a number of books on scientific and philosophical subjects and also displayed an early interest in radical politics. In 1777 he was back in France again and by 1780 was corresponding with Benjamin Franklin. With his political writings he cultivated class consciousness, and urged the execution of the Revolution's enemies. He himself was to fall victim to assassination in 1793, which certainly brought him recognition as a revolutionary martyr in France and the Soviet Union. At first sight, it might appear Weiss was concerning himself with the essential role of the traditional dramatist — that is, the examination of the tragic core of man's plight on earth. Weiss was seemingly to pursue this concern subsequently with dramatized 'case-histories' of Trotsky and Hölderlin and even Kafka (through his stage version of the novel *Der Prozeß*). In all such instances, however, Weiss's primary concern centred on socialist ideas that were or might be associated with those historical figures.

The originally conceived intention was to write a *Hörspiel* where a vision of Revolution could be set in the mind of the historical Marat and everything then viewed as through his eyes:

> Im Mittelpunkt steht die Figur des Marat, der aus der
> Wanne und nur aus seiner Sicht die französischen
> Revolution beschwört. Das Hörspiel ist eine Vision der
> Revolution — so, wie sie sich im Kopf des fiebernden
> Marat abspielt (*14*, p.30)

(It was essentially the format adopted by Weiss in another play later, *Trotzki im Exil*.) In the event Weiss did not carry this notion through in his play on Marat, where the idea of the original projection remains only in the fevered imaginings of Marat (which take us back temporally, in historical fact, to the 1750s), as made physically present on stage in Scene 26 ('Marats Gesichte') in the display of inhumantiy on the part of his teacher, the incomprehension of his own parents, and the personal, philosophical and scientific antagonism of people of the *ancien régime*. If Marat, isolated in his bath on stage, were to be the sole protagonist — historically, he was then at the acme of his political power, the dramatic problem for Weiss would centre on the necessity of overcoming an almost inevitable sense of stasis. In eventually seeing the possibility of introducing a counterweight to Marat, Weiss discovered the chance to give artistic expression to a greatly different viewpoint on the Revolution, one that embraced the notion of an extreme individualism. The counterweight to Marat was of course to be provided by the figure of the Marquis de Sade.

Born in 1740 of aristocratic family, he came to inherit many estates and because of his noble birth belonged to several regiments. He left army life at the end of the Seven Years War, however, for a private life of debauchery and writing, both of which activities brought him into regular trouble with the authorities and resulted in lengthy imprisonments. Weiss incidentally intended originally that, just as Marat has his projected visions, so too should Sade. It was planned that in the debate with Marat on the theme of death and life in Scene 12, there would be projections ranging from medieval torture to a twentieth-century atomic bomb mushroom cloud. In the event Weiss decided against representing Sade's visions on stage.

In the 'Anmerkungen zum geschichtlichen Hintergrund unseres Stückes' Weiss states that his interest in the confrontation of Sade and Marat rested on the

> Konflikt zwischen dem bis zum Äußersten geführten Individualismus und dem Gedanken an eine politische und soziale Umwälzung. Auch Sade war von der Notwendigkeit der Revolution überzeugt und seine Werke sind ein einziger Angriff auf eine korrumpierte herrschende Klasse, jedoch schreckt er auch vor den Gewaltmaßnahmen der Neuordner zurück und sitzt, wie der moderne Vertreter des dritten Standpunkts, zwischen zwei Stühlen. (p.140)

In this sense then Marat and Sade are rather to be seen as types than characters, for both of them do not grow in the course of the play; they have their standpoints that start and remain essentially fixed. Indeed for that very reason the two tend to talk past each other, entrenched as they are in their respective positions and arguments.

After the presentation of both Marat and Sade in the fourth scene by the Herald, homage is paid to Marat in the following scene by the Four Singers who take the side of the people. They recall the course of events over the past four years since the beginning of the downfall of the *ancien régime*, but they do strike a note of discontent, as they bemoan the absence of their rights, that their lot has not noticeably improved. Only in Scene 8 is Marat allowed his first utterance and his concluding words ring out emphatically: 'Ich bin die Revolution.' In the scene Weiss skilfully associates in the mind of the audience the identification of Marat's psychosomatic skin disease with the course of the Revolution:

MARAT
Was ist eine Wanne voll Blut
gegen das Blut das noch fließen wird
Einmal dachten wir daß ein paar hundert Tote

> genügten
> dann sahen wir daß tausende noch zu wenig waren
> und heute sind sie nicht mehr zu zählen
> dort überall
> überall
> (p.26)

The image of the blood-bath and its inevitability is taken up again in Scene 11 ('Triumph des Todes'), in the depiction of the reign of terror. Significantly, Marat here directly addresses the audience off stage, immediately thereby crossing the temporal and the spatial horizons of the play-within-a-play, beyond therefore the on-stage audience of 1808 represented by Coulmier and his family:

MARAT
> *nach vorn sprechend*
> Was jetzt geschieht ist nicht aufzuhalten
> was haben sie nicht alles ertragen
> ehe sie Rache nehmen
> Ihr seht jetzt nur diese Rache
> und denkt nicht daran daß ihr sie dazu triebt
> Jetzt jammert ihr als verspätete Gerechte
> über das Blut das sie vergießen
> doch was ist dieses Blut gegen das Blut
> das sie für euch vergossen haben
> (p.32)

All this time Sade, as director of the inner play, has been content just to observe the proceedings on stage, without interfering even when a degree of unrest springs up amongst the patients. The stage directions inform us that *Sade sitzt unbeweglich, reagiert nicht, überblickt die Bühne mit einem spöttischen Gesichtsausdruck, blickt mit spöttischem Lächeln über die Bühne*. Not until Scene 12 ('Gespräch über Tod und Leben') do Marat and Sade embark upon their dialogue for the first time. Only now do we begin to approach the heart of the matter. For Sade, 'das Prinzip alles Lebendigen [ist] der Tod':

> Und dieser Tod besteht nur in der Einbildung
> ...
> Jeder Tod auch der grausamste
> ertrinkt in der völligen Gleichgültigkeit der Natur
> ...
> Ich hasse die Natur
> ...
> Dieses reglose Zusehn dieses Gesicht aus Eis
> (p.35)

Compared with the execution of Damiens (the would-be assassin of Louis XV), Sade complains, there is now only anonymous, passionless death:

> Unsere Morde haben kein Feuer
> weil sie zur täglichen Ordnung gehören
> Ohne Leidenschaft verurteilen wir
> kein schöner individueller Tod mehr
> stellt sich uns dar
> nur ein anonymes entwertetes Sterben
> in das wir ganze Völker schicken könnten
> in kalter Berechnung
> bis es einmal soweit ist
> alles Leben
> aufzuheben
> (pp.37f.)

Marat retorts that nature's indifference is rather Sade's own apathy, his lack of compassion, but the latter responds that compassion is the property of the privileged and argues that for both of them only extreme actions matter in the end:

Für dich wie für mich
gelten nur die äußersten Extreme

MARAT
Wenn es Extreme sind
dann sind es andere Extreme als deine
Gegen das Schweigen der Natur
stelle ich eine Tätigkeit
In der großen Gleichgültigkeit
erfinde ich einen Sinn
Anstatt reglos zuzusehn
greife ich ein
und ernenne gewisse Dinge für falsch
und arbeite daran sie zu verändern und zu verbessern
Es kommt drauf an
sich am eigenen Haar in die Höhe zu ziehn
sich selbst von innen nach außen zu stülpen
und alles mit neuen Augen zu sehn
(pp.38f.)

Clearly, Marat is quick to contrast their respective extremes, setting action against the indifference of nature and seeking to view the world with fresh eyes. The important words in Marat's speech above are of course 'verändern' and 'verbessern' with their social and political connotation. Unlike Sade, Marat here indicates the sacrificing of his own personality.

Two other scenes then intervene before Marat and Sade are able to pick up the thread of their debate again in Scene 15. Immediately Sade expresses his doubts:

Um zu bestimmen was falsch ist und was recht ist
müssen wir uns kennen
Ich
kenne mich nicht
Wenn ich glaube etwas gefunden zu haben
so bezweifle ichs schon

und muß es wieder zerstören
Was wir tun ist nur ein Traumbild
von dem was wir tun wollen
und nie sind andere Wahrheiten zu finden
als die veränderlichen Wahrheiten der eigenen
Erfahrungen

(pp.44f.)

For him, the only reality is imagination, the world within:

Ich
habe es aufgegeben mich mit ihr zu befassen
mein Leben ist die Imagination
Die Revolution
interessiert mich nicht mehr

Marat disputes such a view, arguing that action is necessary and that one must fight for one's rights and freedom:

mit der Ruhlosigkeit der Gedanken
läßt sich keine Mauer durchbrechen
Mit der Schreibfeder kannst du keine Ordnungen
    umwerfen

(p.48)

The irony of the situation here is that both Sade and Marat realize that the Revolution thus far has not really changed things. We had already been made aware earlier of the sense of frustration at, and dissatisfaction with, the course of the Revolution by the revolutionaries themselves in the shape of the patients' chorus and the Four Singers joining forces in Scene 5 during the homage to Marat:

Marat was ist aus unserer Revolution geworden
Marat wir wolln nicht mehr warten bis morgen
Marat wir sind immer noch arme Leute

> und die versprochenen Änderungen wollen wir heute
> (p.21)

This mood is carried over into Scene 6 ('Erstickte Unruhe'). Now here in Scene 15 Sade points out to Marat in his bath the different worlds of illusion and reality:

> Zusammengekrümmt schwimmst du
> allein mit deinen Vorstellungen von der Welt
> die den Ereignissen draußen nicht mehr entsprechen
> Du wolltest dich einmengen in die Wirklichkeit
> und sie hat dich in die Enge gedrängt
> (pp.47f.)

Marat is forced to acknowledge the shortcomings of the Revolution thus far:

> Wie wir uns auch abmühen das Neue zu fassen
> es entsteht doch erst
> zwischen ungeschickten Handlungen
> So verseucht sind wir von den Gedankengängen
> die Generation von Generation übernahm
> daß auch die besten von uns
> sich immer noch nicht zu helfen wissen
> Wir sind die Erfinder der Revolution
> doch wir können noch nicht damit umgehn
> (p.48)

That constitutes the essential problem. On the other hand, whilst recognizing that the people stand now more oppressed than when they began, Marat still believes the future will bring progress, the improvement in the general social conditions which was the aim of the Revolution. Pertinently, Marat looks across the auditorium at the end of the scene and points to the audience off stage (thereby breaking the time-space barrier once more), and warns against people thinking that the Revolution has already been won. (We note

that Weiss follows this up in the next scene where the patients'
chorus and the Four Singers join forces again to voice their unrest).

The contrasting stances of Sade and Marat are succinctly put in
consecutive lines occurring in Scene 18, when Sade turns his back
on all the nations:

    SADE
        ...
        Ich glaube nur an mich selbst

    MARAT
        sich heftig zu Sade wendend
        Ich glaube nur an die Sache
        die du verrätst
        ...   (p.58)

At the same time, in the next lines, Marat has to admit

        daß es in der Revolution
        um die Interessen von Händlern und Krämern ging
        Die Bourgeoisie
        eine neue siegreiche Klasse
        und darunter der Vierte Stand
        wie immer zu kurz gekommen
                                    (p.59)

In the following scene Sade mocks Marat's continuing belief in
the possibility of justice and equality, arguing rather that in the end
money always dictates the course of power and questioning whether
everyone would subscribe to the notion of being merely another
small cog in a big wheel. Marat in turn knows that unfortunately the
faint-hearted and the fellow-travellers are a part of the Revolution
and have to be cast loose. In the meantime he has to endure the
prospect of such people intriguing and waiting for the chance to
strike.

At last in Scene 21 (over half-way in the numerical sequence
of scenes, but under half-way in the actual text of the play) the
audience is presented with an illustration of Sade's personal sexual
proclivities. There had been evidence of sexual innuendo earlier on
stage, not least in the behaviour of Duperret towards Charlotte
Corday, with which we shall deal later. Sade uses the occasion to
correlate sex, violence and politics, as he bids Corday whip him
whilst he talks to Marat of the Revolution. This act should be seen
by the audience as an example of (Sade's) extreme individualism.
His erotic physical torture and delight is to be equated with the
displays of corporate excess committed by the people in the name of
the Revolution:

> In einer Gesellschaft von Verbrechern
> grub ich das Verbrecherische aus mir selbst hervor
> um es zu erforschen und damit die Zeit zu
>   erforschen
> in der ich lebte
>   (p.69)

We remember how in Scene 12 when Sade and Marat are having
their conversation concerning death and life, Sade, describing the
prolonged sufferings of Damiens under torture, already points to the
sex-violence-politics factor by mentioning Casanova feeling under
the skirts of the ladies watching the process of torture — and at
which juncture Sade looks to the dais where Coulmier and the ladies
are sitting (thus indirectly involving the off-stage audience too).
Here similarly in Scene 21 Weiss's stage directions show that as
Sade offers his bare back to Corday with the whip in her hand, the
ladies on Coulmier's dais stand up expectantly. Quite clearly in this
scene we can understand Weiss's appreciation of Sade's writings to
which he refers in the 'Anmerkungen zum geschichtlichen
Hintergrund unseres Stückes': 'Im *Dialogue entre un prêtre et un
Moribond* und vor allem in *La philosophie dans le Boudoir* wird
jedoch seine dramatische Auffassung deutlich, in der analysierende

und philosophische Dialoge gegen Szenerien körperlicher Exzesse
gestellt werden' (p.140).

Sade reveals how early enthusiasm for the Revolution out of a
spirit of revenge subsided in the face of the horrors unleashed:

> da war dieser Vergeltung schon jeder Sinn
>   genommen
> es war eine mechanische Vergeltung
>
> *Peitschenhieb. Sade krümmt sich zusammen. Corday steht*
> *hochaufgerichtet*
>
> ausgeführt in einer stumpfen Unmenschlichkeit
> in einer eigentümlichen Technokratie
>   (p.71)

and laments that the Revolution is leading

> zu einem Versiechen des einzelnen
> zu einem langsamen Aufgehen in Gleichförmigkeit
> zu einem Absterben des Urteilsvermögens
> zu einer Selbstverleugnung
> zu einer tödlichen Schwäche
> unter einem Staat
> dessen Gebilde unendlich weit
> von jedem einzelnen entfernt ist
> und nicht mehr anzugreifen ist
> Ich kehre mich deshalb ab
>   (p.72)

The very use of the verbal nouns, we note in the first three lines
above, emphasizes the fading of all those energies that are essential
for the success of the Revolution.

But Marat decries the lies and rumours spread about the
Revolution, arguing in Scene 24 the necessity of using force to

achieve success in the struggle. He calls upon the people not to allow themselves to be deflected from the true cause of the Revolution:

> Laßt euch nicht täuschen
> wenn unsre Revolution erstickt worden ist
> und wenn es heißt
> daß die Zustände sich jetzt gebessert haben
> (p.79)

As Marat develops this plea, the stage direction indicates that he turns towards the audience off stage, thus deliberately breaking the inner structural level of time and space, and his language reflects this change with its implied reference to more modern twentieth-century methods of aggression:

> Paßt auf
> denn sobald es ihnen gefällt
> schicken sie euch
> daß ihr ihre Haufen verteidigt
> in Kriege
> deren Waffen in der rapiden Entwicklung
> der gekauften Wissenschaft
> immer schlagkräftiger werden
> und euch in großen Mengen zerreißen
> (pp.80f.)

Marat advances his revolutionary zeal in his address to the National Assembly (in Scene 27, which opens the second act of the play), pointing to the need now for a true, trustworthy and incorruptible deputy:

> Wir haben die Auflösung und das Chaos
> das ist gut
> das ist das erste Stadium
> Jetzt müssen wir zum zweiten Stadium gelangen
> Wählt einen

> der eure Interessen wahrt
> (pp.104f.)

In the circumstances it is tantamount to a call for a dictator, but when the cry rings out 'Marat als Diktator' Marat seemingly recoils:

> Diktator
> dieses Wort soll verschwinden
> ich hasse alles
> was an Meister und Patriarchen erinnert
> ich spreche von einem Chef
> der in der Zeit der Krise
> (p.105)

Here the stage direction pointedly indicates that Marat's words are drowned in the mighty tumult.

Marat's intention in the following scene to dictate his 14th of July Call to the Nation provides the opportunity for Marat and Sade to reflect respectively on their function as writer, and to consider where it has led them. Sade calls upon Marat to give up his writing:

> Gib es auf Marat
> du sagtest selbst
> es sei nichts zu erreichen mit dem Gekritzel
> Auch ich habe mein Hauptwerk längst aufgegeben
> eine dreißig Meter lange Papierrolle
> dicht beschrieben mit winziger Schrift
> damals im Kerker
> Sie verschwand beim Fall der Bastille
> (p.109)

Marat retorts that he has always written with action in mind:

> Wenn ich schrieb
> so schrieb ich immer mit dem Gedanken an
>   Handlung

> hatte immer vor Augen
> daß dies nur Vorbereitung war
> Wenn ich schrieb
> so schrieb ich immer im Fieber
> und hörte schon das Dröhnen der Handlungen
> (p.110)

Again, Sade mockingly calls on Marat to give up ('Vergiß deinen Aufruf/er enthält nur Lügen'). Pointing to the Four Singers who are sitting around waiting as 'lost revolutionaries', Sade wonders where the Revolution is leading. 'Poor' Marat even gives voice to his own doubts:

> Warum wird alles so undeutlich
> Alles was ich sagte
> war doch durchdacht und wahr
> jedes Argument stimmte
> warum zweifle ich jetzt
> warum klingt alles falsch
> (p.112)

Nowhere else in the play does Weiss demonstrate so clearly as in this twenty-eighth scene a sense of affinity existing between the two protagonists. Sade — he of the licentious behaviour, the writer of obscene books — is the highly individualistic figure censored, banned, imprisoned. His abandoned masterpiece to which he refers in the scene is the highly graphic and explicit sexual tome *One Hundred and Twenty Days of Sodom* which represents in effect a challenge to the accepted sexual mores of the society and authority of the day by opening up a world seemingly free of restraints. Relevantly at this point we recall the remark of Peter Weiss made in the autobiographical novel *Fluchtpunkt* (1962) about the impact on him on reading Henry Miller's *Tropic of Cancer* and how the revolt against authority expressed in the spirit of sexual rebellion and freedom in its pages 'hit him in the face'. Sade the artist is dependent on his imagination (even if corrupt), the liberation of his mind. As he says in Scene 30:

> Marat
> diese Gefängnisse des Innern
> sind schlimmer als die tiefsten steinernen Verliese
> und solange sie nicht geöffnet werden
> bleibt all euer Aufruhr
> nur eine Gefängnisrevolte
> die niedergeschlagen wird
> von bestochenen Mitgefangenen
>   (pp.123f.)

But Sade's cells of the mind can be unlocked by his sexual fantasies. In that sense they create for him a revolutionary drive. By the same token, Marat's own revolutionary zeal, that demanded an excess of killing, may be seen, at least in part, as a form of ego-gratification of blood-letting. We remember Sade's words at the end of Scene 27, the meeting of the National Assembly where Marat, as friend of the people, had urged yet more repressive measures and gained for himself dictatorial powers:

> Einen werden sie finden
> Auf den sie alles abladen können
> und sie werden ihn ernennen zu einem blutgierigen
>   Ungeheuer
> das in die Geschichte eingehen kann
> unter dem Namen Marat
>   (p.107)

And in the Epilogue Corday points to the revolutionary path to freedom that the sanguinary Marat, proceeding from Rousseau, had pursued: 'doch für dich gings zur Freiheit über einen Berg von Leichen' (p.132).

Sade finds himself in Charenton, confined at Napoleon's command. As has been earlier noted, the Director encourages him to put on plays for the therapeutic benefit of the patients. At the same time Sade makes us aware of the threat of censorship hanging over him even here. Certainly we are aware that Sade's piece on Marat now being performed has been subject to the excision of lines and even parts of scenes, as Coulmier makes clear from time to time when unrest grows amongst the patients. And Sade himself refers to this danger of censorship when asking Marat in Scene 28 how the latter will cope in the changing times: 'Oder willst du daß einer über dich bestimmt/und über deine geschriebenen Worte' (p.112).

Of course Marat's writings had in turn also got him into trouble with the authorities. This is already suggested in the brief exchange between Marat and Simonne in Scene 26:

> MARAT
> Simonne
> wo sind meine alten Manuskripte
> die Abenteuer des Potovsky
> und die Polnischen Briefe
> und meine Schrift über die Ketten der Sklaverei
>
> SIMONNE
> *abwehrend*
> Laß doch das Zeug
> es bringt dich nur ins Verderben
> (p.90)

Marat himself makes reference again to his early work *The Chains of Slavery*, which was immediately suppressed, as well as to the later pamphlets:

> Dies gehörte ja dazu
> immer standen sie bereit
> meine Aussagen abzufangen
> zu verleumden und unschädlich zu machen
> Nach jeder Fertigstellung eines Flugblatts

mußte ich hinunter in die Laufgänge
(p.111)

Writing, Marat feels (as he tells Sade in Scene 28), is but the preparation for action, never the end in itself. This was as valid for him as scientist (with his scientific treatises) and thinker (with his philosophical essays) as for his later virulent, revolutionary journalistic pieces (he was founder-editor of *L'Ami du peuple* which undoubtedly helped to provoke the massacres of September 1792; the sensationalist daily finished incidentally the day after Marat died). It is important that we note the sequence of events that leads Marat to the Revolution, as described by the characters who have appeared on stage in Scene 26 as physical projections of Marat's mind:

> *Die Figuren nehmen die Haltung von Richtern ein, die ein Urteil aussprechen.*

VOLTAIRE
Und als er es mit seiner Forscherei zu nichts brachte

PRIESTER
Da kam diesem Dilettanten die Revolution gerade
  gelegen

LEHRER
Und er ging zu den Unterdrückten über

NEUREICHER
Und nannte sich Freund des Volkes

PRIESTER
Doch er dachte nicht an das Volk

LAVOISIER
Sondern nur an seine eigene Unterdrücktheit
(p.94)

Marat's political life is in reality the fruit of bitter personal rejection. Only after he has been rejected as a scientist (Marat felt he deserved more recognition than Newton), as thinker (and mirrored in the scorn poured on him by Lavoisier and Voltaire in this Scene 26), and suffering the imputation that he was a quack, does he throw in his lot with the people (though the suggestion above of an individualistic motivation at work would seem at variance with the earlier conveyed perception that Marat had abandoned his own personality for the sake of the people).

Both men then, Marat and Sade, are part of society, privileged society: the former, doctor by profession and mixing in well-to-do circles; the latter, aristocrat, son of a diplomat and inheritor of vast estates. Yet they are both in their respective ways outcasts. They each react against that society, with Marat turning to political violence and Sade to sexual violence. And now both of them are victims of and sacrifices to the times in which they live and have helped to shape. Each is respectively creator of a form of violence before which he must inevitably and inexorably bow. Having pronounced himself friend of the people and having been criticized by them for failing to deliver, Marat falls prey to the monster that is the Revolution. Sade has freedom of the mind, of the imagination, but his writings have put him into Charenton. He can write and put on plays at Charenton, but they and he are subject to Coulmier's censorship (even if some censored material does creep back in unauthorized). He may seem to dictate the course of events in his play, getting Corday to kill Marat on stage — as happened in history. But he does not have ultimate control which is Coulmier's. Sade cannot dictate physically in any positive sense in Charenton, being dominant only in the mind that is reflected sexually and in anarchically theatrical fashion. Indeed physically on stage he is dominated by Corday herself. Sade then is a creator, but at the same time a victim, of his obscene works. And even if he chooses mockingly to ignore Coulmier and laugh triumphantly at the end of his play — the triumph of his play that reflects his knowledge of the course of the Revolution, it is but a play, no more (for him, as of course for all the characters). Reality for him is to stay a prisoner in the asylum to his death in 1814. Marat is a prisoner of the Revolution, symbolically in his bath that becomes his deathbed and coffin after his assassination by Charlotte Corday, the victim of the *réaction thermidorienne*.

5. Other Characters

Roux

Weiss tells us in the 'Anmerkungen zum geschichtlichen Hintergrund unseres Stückes' that Roux is 'eine der fesselndsten Persönlichkeiten der Revolution', and that his function in the play is that of 'eines Ansporners und Zuspitzers, eines Alter Ego, an dem Marats Thesen sich messen lassen' (p.143). For the purpose of the play, Weiss chooses not to heed the historical fact that in the last days before his death Marat turned from Roux and condemned him too to death. In reality, after Marat's murder, Roux was imprisoned for his extreme views on social reform. A former constitutional cleric turned radical revolutionary, he denounced the laws which had been made by the rich for the rich.

On stage he is seen to be wearing a form of straitjacket, thus impeding his freedom of movement, but his radicalism emerges forcefully enough through his vocal urgings of the people, in short his rabble-rousing. His mere presentation by the Herald in Scene 4 is sufficient to cause the director of the asylum to raise a threatening finger. The Herald makes it clear that Roux has been 'jailed' for his political radicalism — a form of political madness, as it were (just as Sade has been interned for his form of sexual madness). Also made clear at the outset is the fact that Roux's lines have already been heavily censored:

> Leider hat die Zensur sehr viel
> gestrichen von seinen Aussagen im Spiel
> denn sie gingen in ihrem Ton zu weit

> für die Ordnungsbewahrer in unserer Zeit
> (p.16)

Roux has his first opportunity to stoke the fires of unrest in Scene 6 ('Erstickte Unruhe'), holding, the stage direction informs us, centre stage:

> Wer beherrscht die Markthallen
> Wer hält die Speicher verschlossen
> Wer hat die Reichtümer aus den Schlössern ergattert
> Wer sitzt auf den Ländereien
> die an uns verteilt werden sollten
> (p.22)

Roux is pulled back by a sister, but he has made his point and the unrest grows, causing Coulmier to intervene.

Roux does not appear again until Scene 19, but this and the following one are his major scenes. His agitating exhortation is a call to arms:

> Greift zu den Waffen
> kämpft um euer Recht
> Wenn ihr euch jetzt nicht holt was ihr braucht
> dann könnt ihr noch ein Jahrhundert lang warten
> und zusehn
> was die sich für einen Betrieb errichten
> (p.60)

As the Herald points out (p.61), Roux has indeed exchanged the pulpit for the streets, changed the heavenly fields for more earthy or earthly images. He is restrained but briefly and soon is on his feet again shouting his demands for food for the poor, the public ownership of workshops and factories, and, above all — and this is an impassioned outcry of pacifism — an end to the war. The patient playing the part of Roux has here reinstituted lines that had originally been censored, as an incensed Coulmier makes very clear to Sade at this point that the scene had in fact been cut. Violent outburst is met with force and Roux is overpowered and led away.

It is hardly a surprise that the one apologist who steps forward to defend Marat, after the latter has been subjected to a barrage of scorn by a range of characters from his past (who appear on stage in Scene 26 as a projection of Marat's mind) should be Roux. He quickly foments unrest, but noteworthy is the verbal force of the language of the stage directions to indicate the activity immediately to follow: *Coulmier springt auf. Schwestern und Pfleger laufen auf Roux zu und reißen ihn zum Hintergrund zurück* (p.96). Action on the part of Roux sparks reaction on the part of the Director and the attendants.

We observe then that Roux, the political agitator, concerns himself solely with the actual political situation. To him fall the final words of the play to deliver, words directed not only at the patients and on-stage audience in the asylum, but also, more significantly, at the audience off-stage: 'Wann werdet ihr sehen lernen/Wann werdet ihr endlich verstehen' (p.136). At this point the stage direction indicates that Roux is swallowed up in the serried ranks of the frenzied inmates chanting and at the mercy of their mad march-like dance, and disappears from sight. In his radicalism Roux has been seen to outstrip even Marat, to represent the notion of total revolutionary overthrow. This time at least the attempt has failed.

Duperret and Charlotte Corday

If Marat is leader of the extreme Montagnards, Duperret and Charlotte Corday are seen as members of the more moderate Republicans, the Girondins, who come into conflict with the more radical faction in the Convention and are indeed overthrown in June 1793, thus leading to reprisals, including the assassination of Marat. The good-looking, twenty-four-year-old Charlotte Corday comes to Paris from Caen to avenge the Girondin leaders who are arrested or forced to flee. Amongst those she names in Scene 30 are Louvet, Pétion, Vergniaud and Brissot, whose journal — 'libre, impartial et national' — *La Patriote français* (1789-1793) reflected their conflict with the Montagnards in the later numbers.

Weiss admits in the 'Anmerkungen zum geschichtlichen Hintergrund unseres Stückes' that he has taken liberties in the portrayal of Duperret who was a Girondin deputy (p.143). Historically, he was on Marat's black list and his brief association with Corday certainly assured his place under the guillotine. Here in the play Weiss shows Duperret more as a type, a representative of those moderate Republicans of the time, championing the cause of the Revolution.

Not until Scene 17 is Duperret given his first speaking lines in his first conversation with Corday. Here he makes the classic error of its kind in underestimating an opponent — in this case Marat:

> Du sprichst von Marat
> Doch wer ist Marat
> irgendein hergelaufener Corsikaner Verzeihung
>   Sardinier
> oder gar Jude
> Wer hört ihm schon zu
> Nur das Gesindel auf den Gassen
> Dieser Marat ist für uns nicht gefährlich
>   (p.53)

For her part, however, Corday is well aware of Marat's intentions:

> Marat sollte ernannt werden zum Tribun und
>   Diktator
> Noch heuchelt er daß die Maßnahmen der Gewalt
> nur von begrenzter Dauer wären
> wir aber wissen
> daß Auflösung und Gesetzlosigkeit sein Ziel ist
>   (p.53)

Duperret feels there is no need to flee and therefore fails to heed

Corday's warning to leave Paris while he can:

> Und warum sollte ich fliehn
> jetzt da es nicht mehr lange dauern kann
> ...
> Sie können sich nicht mehr lange halten
> diese Emporkömmlinge und Fanatiker
> die keinen Weitblick haben keine Kultur
> Nein Charlotte ich bleibe hier
>
> und warte auf den Tag
> an dem wir das Wort Freiheit
> wieder aussprechen dürfen
>
> (pp.55f.)

Duperret's blindness to the real stituation, his resolve to stay in Paris at this time is compounded on stage by the infatuation of the inmate playing Duperret for the woman playing the part of Charlotte Corday. Already in the presentation of the characters in Scene 4 Duperret is seen to approach the beautiful Corday ('eine in die Augen fallende Erscheinung'), pawing her furtively. It is an action in itself that further illustrates the stripping of stage illusion. During the first conversation between the two in Scene 17, the stage direction reads: *Duperret benützt die Szene, um Corday liebkosend über den Körper zu streichen* (p.52). Duperret's action causes the Herald to intervene: 'Nütz deine Rolle nicht aus/deine Liebe ist platonisch'. Indeed Weiss points out in the 'Anmerkungen zum geschichtlichen Hintergrund unseres Stückes' (p.143) that, historically, Duperret had not been Corday's lover, that favour falling rather to a certain M. Tournelis who fled from Caen to join 'les gens de Coblentz'. But Sade and Weiss have an erotomaniac play the part of Duperret and this serves Weiss's purpose very well indeed in that it enables him, on the one hand, to suggest the sexual proclivities of Sade again, and, on the other, to show through Duperret's constant sexual advances to Corday on stage (to the extent that he even fluffs his lines; in general, we should note the stage directions throughout that scene, pp.51-56) the absurdity of his views on the current state of political affairs. His unfulfilled sexual excesses undermine his spoken thoughts on harmony, culture and moderation and highlight the inherent grotesqueness of the situation. In addition to the sexual rejection by Corday, who has a mission to fulfil, he is also spurned politically (as a Girondin) by Marat and put on his black list. He lives in false hopes, has dreams which turn out to be a nightmare.

His second conversation with Corday occurs immediately after the scene of Marat's persecution and is to provide, as the Herald reminds the audience, an illustration of the sunny side of life. The patent irony here is heightened in that the interaction between the two in this Scene 23 is carried out in a quasi-operatic style (to which we shall later refer). The two of them look forward to the day when men will live together in harmony, when there will be equal human rights, when a higher order of society shall exist (pp.77f.). But whilst their language mouths in aria style the noble ideals of 'Einklang', 'Freiheit', 'Grundvertrag', 'höhere Ordnung', 'Übereinkunft', 'Recht', Duperret's sexual advances become progessively uncontrolled (*über ihr Haar streichend*; *die Hand unter Cordays Kleid schiebend*; *versucht, Corday auf den Mund zu küssen; Corday festhaltend und sie mit Liebkosungen überschüttend*). The nobility of thought is lost entirely — and deliberately so — in the exaggerated theatricality of the mode of delivery and accompanying action.

Even when Duperret is not so directly involved in the action in the play-within-a-play, the audience is still made aware of his presence and his erotomania. At the meeting of the National Assembly (in Scene 27), where important political argument develops that will lead to far-reaching revolutionary action, Duperret is to be seen sitting in the Girondin ranks between two patients who behave as prostitutes. His brief verbal intervention of Marat's impassioned address to the Assembly is predictable:

> O hätten wir noch schöpferische Gedanken
> anstelle von Agitation
> Hätten wir wieder Schönheit und Harmonie

anstatt Taumel und Fanatismus
(pp.105f.)

His very employment of the subjunctive reflects the fatuousness of his exclamation against the actualities of life conveyed through Marat's use of the indicative. Duperret is swiftly and forcibly silenced at this juncture by the Four Singers.

During the preparations for Corday's third visit (in Scene 29) Duperret bids her wake from *her* nightmare (for, with eyes closed, she has been describing step-by-step the act of execution by the guillotine — though she also goes on to allude, at a further level of statement directed to contemporary audiences, to later atrocities to be perpetrated by the Nazis ['Es ist jetzt die Rede von Backofenschüben/und sie werden abgeholt nach Listen', p.117]):

wach auf Charlotte und betrachte die Bäume
betrachte das rosige Abendlicht
und denke an solche Dinge nicht
verspüre die Wärme und sommerliche Luft
in der sich hebt deine schöne Brust
(p.115)

The grotesque juxtaposition here of the beauties of nature with its life-giving force and the evils of the guillotine with its death-bringing violence echoes of course the similar association briefly made in the song and mime of Corday's arrival in Paris on the 11th July (in Scene 10). There she buys a dagger (for the purpose of killing Marat) — again there is the innuendo of sex and violence, for the stage direction follows: *Der Verkäufer schaut ihr in den Busen und beschreibt eine Gebärde der Bewunderung* (p.30). Momentarily Corday hears the birds singing in the Tuileries, catches the scent of the flowers before she takes herself to the streets 'wo der Geruch der Blumen sich mit dem Geruch des Bluts vermischte', to the streets of Paris where now a nightmarish dance of death denoting the unleashing of the terror takes place to conclude the scene. Here in Scene 29, pursuant to his words above, Duperret strokes Corday's breast and, in so doing, he also feels the shape of that very dagger she is trying to conceal. Having earlier refused to heed Corday's advice to leave Paris — he does not wish to leave her — he himself now beseeches Corday that they should both flee to Caen forthwith. Only now does *he* wake up to the nightmare reality of what lies ahead. But it is — historically speaking — already too late.

Corday will not heed him, will not be deflected from her 'divine' mission. From a minor Norman landed-gentry family, Charlotte Corday d'Armont from Caen, descended from a sister of Corneille, was a liberal Girondin idealist, who, following the overthrow of the Girondins in the Convention on 19 June 1793, came to Paris to seek revenge. Her role in the events of the day certainly attracted the attention of German writers and already by the turn of that century Wieland and Jean Paul Richter had both written pieces on and about Charlotte Corday. Her deed then is that of delivering the people from the hand of oppression, Marat. Schooled in the convent at Caen 'in der ekstatischen Versunkenheit', she goes her way thinking only of Joan of Arc and the biblical Judith, as Weiss reminds us in the 'Anmerkungen zum geschichtlichen Hintergrund unseres Stückes' (p.143). Now the Herald had already introduced a religious dimension by introducing a reference to Calvary into the context of Roux's first rabble-rousing exploit in Scene 19, when describing the latter's role as Marat's apostle:

> und stellt ihnen Marat als Heiligen hin
> denn das verspricht schon einen Gewinn
> weil dieser wie ein Gekreuzigter ist
> *zeigt auf Marat*
> und daran erbaut sich jeder Christ
> (p.62)

And there is no doubt but that Corday sees her mission as 'religious', for during the preparations for her third visit to the door of Marat's house in Scene 29 she makes actual mention of Judith:

In meinem Zimmer in Caen
auf dem Tisch unterm offenen Fenster
liegt Judiths aufgeschlagenes Buch
Judith brach auf um nie zurückzukehren
Angetan mit wunderbarer Schönheit
trat sie vor das Lager
des Tyrannen
und mit einem einzigen Hieb
vernichtete sie ihn

(p.116)

We may briefly remind ourselves from the *Book of Judith* in the Apocrypha that the beautiful Judith, widow of Manasses, saves the besieged city of Bethulia from foreign conquest by slaying the enemy Holofernes in his tent after pretending to be physically attracted to him. This biblical theme had been the subject of literary attention long before Weiss, not least in the case of the nineteenth-century dramatist Friedrich Hebbel who wrote his powerful five-act drama on Judith in 1841. Like Hebbel's Judith, so too Weiss's Corday exudes an air of sexuality and violence as well as an aura of innocence and virtue. Attention is drawn to these latter qualities and to a sense of decorum already in the presentation by the Herald in Scene 4: 'und bindet sich gerade das Brusttuch zu' (the flimsy white cloth that serves to conceal her bosom which her blouse would otherwise expose, p.14) and again later in Scene 17 when Corday and Duperret have their first conversation (with the mention of 'Kloster' and 'Tugend') and Duperret bids her return to Caen:

Ach liebste Corday
kehre zurück in den Kreis deiner frommen
    Freundinnen
und führe ein Leben in Zurückgezogenheit und in
    Gebeten
denn du bist ihnen denen du hier begegnest
nicht gewachsen

(p.53)

Yet her lips have a certain suggestiveness ('sinnlich geschwungen und zart', p.76) and gradually we are made conscious of an air of sexuality in her contact in turn with each of the three men, Sade, Duperret and Marat. As we have earlier noted, in the case of Duperret, the expression of sexual desire is entirely his. For her part, in pursuit of her planned murder of Marat, she consistently ignores or spurns Duperret's advances — ultimately, be it noted, forcibly rejecting him on the occasion of her third and last visit to Marat:

DUPERRET
    Was willst du von ihm
    kehre um Charlotte
    fällt vor ihr aufs Knie

CORDAY
    Ich habe einen Auftrag
    den muß ich ausführen
    Geh
    stößt ihn mit dem Fuß
    und laß mich allein
    Duperret umschlingt ihre Beine. Sie tritt mehrmals nach
    ihm. Duperret zieht sich auf den Knien zurück.
                                                                    (p.119)

She literally stands over Duperret who is — not for the first time (cf. stage directions in Scene 22, p.76) — grovelling at her feet and she scornfully thrusts him aside. She can therefore be said to be dominant over the good-natured yet pathetic Duperret. Certainly she is dominant over Sade in Scene 21 where sexuality and violence are nakedly displayed — literally so — in her flogging of Sade at his behest as he talks to Marat of the Revolution. The rhythmic blows from the whip force Sade to his knees and then to the ground as Corday straddles him. But it is in her murderous pursuit of Marat that we can trace the most prolonged and orchestrated build-up as for the act of sex.

In her very first visit to Marat in Scene 9, for example, she voices her intention to thrust the dagger between Marat's ribs, let us note, in amorous tones (*im Ton einer Liebeserklärung*), which grow intense and obsessive (*besessen*). Sexual innuendo and violent intent are observable at the outset. When she comes to Marat's door for the third and last time in Scene 30, it is Sade who makes a series of innuendoes to Marat to arouse sexual desire, with the mention of Corday as virgin (though seemingly a knowing virgin), the innocence of convent girls. His reference to the dagger at this juncture is merely suggestive of the possibility of love-play.

> Marat
> was sind alle Pamphlete und Reden
> gegen sie
> die da steht und zu dir will
> um dich zu küssen und zu umarmen
> Marat
> eine Virgo Intacta steht vor dir und bietet sich dir an
> ...
> Sieh
> da steht sie
> mit nackter Brust unterm dünnen Tuch
> Vielleicht trägt sie ein Messer
> zur Aufreizung des Liebesspiels
> *Corday bewegt sich einen Schritt näher an die Wanne*
> *heran. Sie bietet ihren Körper dar, wiegt sich leicht hin und*
> *her...*
>
> (pp.120f.)

The patients now step forward to perform the 'copulation' mime, whilst Sade couples the ideas of sexual and political violence, a cry immediately taken up and repeated by the Chorus on two further occasions in the scene:

> Denn was wäre schon diese Revolution
> ohne eine allgemeine Kopulation
> (p.122)

As Corday approaches Marat in his bath, Sade himself seems aroused (...*und die Handlung voller Spannung verfolgt*, p.125). Her movements are as in love foreplay: *Ihre linke Hand hält sie wie zu Liebkosungen ausgestreckt*; *Sie führt ihre linke Hand nah an seiner Haut über seine Brust, seine Schultern, seinen Hals.* Her right hand concealed is holding the dagger. This whole performance assumes an added air of insanity when we remember that the role of Corday is being played by a somnambulist patient who because of her condition succeeds in bringing an element of unreality to her act of assassination. Nor do we forget the look on her distorted face as she names the Girondin members at Caen to Marat: *Während des Aussprechens der Namen verzerrt sich ihr Gesicht mehr und mehr zu einer Wildheit, in der sich Haß und Wollust mischen* (the above stage directions are all to be found on p.126).

Precisely at the moment when Corday raises the dagger to strike, Sade and Weiss skilfully freeze the action by having the Herald blow shrilly on his whistle. The latter indicates that it is Sade's intent deliberately to interrupt the climax as part of his dramatic plan to enable Marat — and by definition the off-stage audience too — to discover the course of history over the fifteen years from the death of Marat to the year 1808, the time of the play's performance. The very title of this new scene 'Interruptus' emphasizes for good measure the sexual implications of the foregoing act. The assassination ensues immediately in Scene 32 where she stands — again, dominant — over Marat in his bath, and sexuality and violence are further linked by the stage direction indicating that Corday is immediately seized by the Four Singers (representing the people) who force her arms back until her breasts are exposed (p.130).

Corday's role is to serve the Girondin cause, that of Simonne Evrard to serve Marat — on a personal level: the latter's occasional tyrannical outbursts (eg. pp.25, 104f.) at Simonne incidentally are to be regarded as an extension of his public revolutionary outpourings. Corday's act of murder, however, shows in itself the very continuation of the principle of Revolution. And whilst she may historically outlive Marat, it is but for a token time, for she was guillotined on 17 July 1793. But what she is seen to stand for — as against the radicalism unleashed in the reign of terror, as against the extreme individualism of Sade — is the voice of moderation expressed in the social and political views of the Girondins (which many Germans found favourable at least in the early stages of the Revolution). As she argues in the Epilogue (Scene 33), both she and Marat proceeded from Rousseau, but whilst both wanted freedom, the respective means chosen to achieve it were different. Claiming she would do the same again, her high liberal ideal is sustained to the end (p.133).

Yet we might consider that within the framework of the play Corday's display of this high liberal ideal is in one deliberate sense a flawed portrayal. Her views that culminate in her mission to assassinate Marat arguably lose a certain validity by the air of unreality that the somnambulist brings to the role of Corday (thereby emphasizing the 'playacting'). Her very behaviour, her falling in and out of a role, leads us to look critically at the character and action of Corday. Indeed the idiosyncratic behaviour of each of the patients playing roles in the play makes for the possibility of flaws not only in the presentation of the characters but also of ideas relevant to those characters. The erotomaniac spoils the import of Duperret's noble words on harmony and freedom. It is generally conceded that, historically, Marat's psychosomatic condition probably accentuated his attitude to life that encouraged the reign of terror, and the paranoiac playing the role of Marat (over-)sharpens that image by his performance. By the same token Sade himself is forced to admit in the Epilogue that his play has no satisfactory conclusion and he is left with his doubts, knowing only that his own form of revolutionary zeal conditioned by his individual sexual excesses is not the answer. In short, by portraying the social and political upheavals of revolutionary France at the end of the eighteenth century and in the early years of the nineteenth against a backcloth of insanity in the shape of the Asylum of Charenton, with inmates playing the character roles, Weiss persuasively and spectacularly brings into focus and into question the very rationality of life.

Coulmier

In some respects Coulmier may be seen as the most interesting character on stage after Marat and Sade. He was originally a Premonstratensian monk and a Deputy to the National Assembly. As director of the asylum at Charenton, he was, by all historical accounts, a kind man basically liked by the inmates. He certainly did permit Sade to put on some plays and seems to have interceded with the outside authorities on Sade's behalf from time to time. In the play he is made to appear as more an oppressor and upholder of the Napoleonic order: *er nimmt gern eine napoleonische Haltung ein*, we learn from Weiss's description of the character at the start. Dressed as he is in elegant clothing, coat and top hat, he stands out even from Sade, whose clothing, whilst of good quality (*vornehm*), is worn (*doch verkommen*), not to mention the patients who wear their asylum attire with some modifications to take account of the roles that they play, and the attendants. This sense of apartness is further emphasized by the richness of dress worn by Coulmier's wife and daughter, who accompany him to watch the performance. Their separateness is also manifested — physically — in the level of structure. As the audience of the inner play, they are seated on a raised tribunal to one side of the stage. (By the same token, being an audience, they also have an affinity with us, the contemporary theatre-goers. The on-stage audience serves to involve the off-stage audience in an active sense as participants in the events enacted on stage, whilst at the same time emphasizing for us the theatrical illusion going on before our eyes.) Coulmier sits on the same side of the stage as Sade, it should be noted. And it is the Director who in the Prologue gets the proceedings of the play under way by delivering a greeting to the spectators who have come to watch Sade's play. He explains that as Director he feels the plays can be

therapeutically beneficial for the patients who act out these pieces by
Sade. He sees Charenton as modern and enlightened:

> Als moderne und aufgeklärte Leute
> sind wir dafür daß bei uns heute
> die Patienten der Irrenanstalt
> nicht mehr darben unter Gewalt
> sondern sich in Bildung und Kunst betätigen
> somit die Grundsätze bestätigen
> die wir einmal im feierlichen Dekret
> der Menschenrechte für immer geprägt
>
> (p.12)

Nevertheless as director of the institution with responsibility
for order and discipline, Coulmier is concerned about the tone of the
piece and its presentation. As the Herald reminds us, in Scene 4,
Coulmier has seen to it that a lot of Roux's rabble-rousing lines have
already been censored from the play (p.16) and he wags his finger in
warning to Roux as soon as the latter opens his mouth. Coulmier's
first real sign of unease occurs in Scene 6 ('Erstickte Unruhe') when
the patients become agitated at Roux's words. The stage directions
are informative: *Coulmier springt von seinem Stuhl auf*; *Coulmier
sieht sich um*; *klopft mit dem Stock auf den Boden*. He addresses
Sade (who pointedly ignores him), calling for calm and claiming to
act as the voice of reason (against the voice of unreason of Roux and
the patients who have been crying out for a fairer deal and freedom).
Coulmier draws attention to the different temporal structures with
the reminder that it is 1808, not 1793, and that things have changed
(and by implication the third time level of the present is here
included):

> Ich sehe ich muß hier die Stimme der Vernunft
>   vertreten
> Wie soll denn das werden wenn wir schon am
>   Anfang des Stückes
> soviel Unruhe aufkommen lassen

> Ich muß doch um etwas Besänftigung bitten
> Schließlich sind heute andere Zeiten als damals
> und wir sollten uns bemühen
> die längst überwundenen Mißstände
> in einem etwas verklärten Schimmer zu sehen
>
> (pp.22f.)

Coulmier remains seated then until Scene 11 ('Triumph des Todes'),
but jumps up once more as the executions are mimed on stage, to
complain again to Sade that all this is upsetting the patients and
cannot be called education ('so geht das nicht/das können wir nicht
Erbauung nennen', p.33). Again, Sade fails to respond. Indeed the
Herald even interrupts Coulmier to bid the audience — ironically,
because different time levels are here involved: the comment is valid
not only for the 1808 situation, but also for contemporary theatre-
goers — to watch calmly the barbarous goings-on

> weil wir die Taten von damals verachten
> Denn an Einsicht sind wir heute viel klüger
> als jene deren Zeit für immer vorüber
>
> (pp.33f.)

A third complaint to Sade is voiced two scenes later in 'Marats
Liturgie' over Marat's outburst against the Church. Clearly, some
agreed censoring of the passage has, in the event, been ignored and
as upholder of bourgeois moral values, of State and Church,
Coulmier sees the necessity here to emphasize how things have
improved under the Napoleonic regime — the time difference
therefore between 1793 and 1808 again highlighted here:

> Wie nimmt sich denn sowas heute aus
> da unser Kaiser von kirchlichen Würdenträgern
>   umgeben ist
> und es sich immer aufs neue zeigt
> wie sehr das Volk des priesterlichen Trostes bedarf
> Von einer Unterdrückung kann überhaupt keine

Rede sein
Im Gegenteil da wird alles getan um die Not zu
  lindern
mit Kleidereinsammlung Krankenhilfe und
  Suppenverteilung
und auch wir hier unterstehen nicht nur der Gnade
der weltlichen Regierung
sondern vor allem der Gunst und dem Verständnis
unsrer geistlichen Väter

(p.42)

But we note that, as in Scene 11, so too here it is the Herald who has the last word.

Coulmier is quickly on his feet again in the next scene at the regrettable intervention of the patient, and in Scene 18 feels obliged to call a warning when Sade turns his back on all nations. Not surprisingly Roux's first agitating address in the following scene soon has Coulmier on his feet once more protesting:

Sollen wir uns so was mit anhören
wir Bürger eines neuen Zeitalters
wir die den Aufschwung wollen

(p.61)

As Roux develops his revolutionary theme of protest in Scene 20, Coulmier's own reactions become the more marked: *Coulmier fuchtelt mit den Händen und erhebt Einspruch*; *Coulmier läuft von der Tribüne hinunter zu Sade*; *sich heftig an Sade wendend* (pp.65f.). Complain as Coulmier may at what he sees as Roux's defeatist talk of pacifism and at the unauthorized reintroduction of a censored scene, Sade yet again chooses to ignore him. The same lack of reaction from Sade faces Coulmier in Scene 24 initially at least, before Sade relents and calms the Director's worries over Marat's words to the people not to be taken in by the promise that things would now be better when the Revolution has been stamped out.

At the start of the second act in the scene of the National Assembly Coulmier cannot contain his displeasure any longer and vigorously defends Perregaux the banker, denounced by Marat (p.101). Shortly afterwards he calls upon Marat and the others to remember that the year is 1808 and that some of the people denounced have in fact been restored to favour by Napoleon (p.104). In short, Coulmier puts the Revolution into some perspective when the tumult grows in the Assembly, lifting it out of the temporal structure of the inner play to merge with the second (and by implication the third) time level. Similarly in the Epilogue (scene 33, where the marked-out spatial and temporal structures also merge) Coulmier reminds us of the changed times and that the signs for the future look bright. For the off-stage audience of course there resides a certain irony in Coulmier's words, for as Marat could not know of the events to follow after his death in 1793 (save through the artifice of the musical historical revue provided in Scene 31), so too could Coulmier not foresee the course of history after 1808, the year of the performance of Sade's play at Charenton. His vision of victory therefore looks misplaced in the light of events to befall Napoleon and France after 1811.

Throughout, Coulmier sees himself as the voice of moderation and enlightenment at Charenton; one result of which of course is that the inmates — and not least Sade — try the Director's patience over censored passages in the play, for example, and do not heed his views. Coulmier's views in fact may be seen as conventional expression and certainly do not have the same ring of serious, impassioned intent as conveyed by the addresses of Marat and Roux, to whose chagrin, however, the Revolution had thus far not affected changes as sufficiently and as properly as they would have wished and for which they had indeed hoped:

> Jetzt aber leben wir in ganz anderen Zeiten
> ohne Unterdrücker und ohne Pleiten
> wir sind auf dem Wege uns zu erholen
> wir haben Brot und es gibt auch Kohlen
> und haben wir auch noch einen Krieg

> so leuchtet vor uns doch nur der Sieg
>
> (p.134)

The orchestra at this juncture begins to play the final march and a banner bearing an idealized portrait of Napoleon is let down. The music grows louder as does the rhythmic stamping of feet of the patients marching — to tumultuous, uncontrollable proportions. Little wonder that the stage direction reads: *Coulmier tritt beunruhigt zur Seite und winkt mit den Armen ab* (p.135). The Director makes a token appeal of loyalty to the Emperor, France and Charenton, but his call is superseded by the rhythmic shouts of the patients who for one final time embrace sex, violence and politics:

> Charenton Charenton
> Napoleon Napoleon
> Nation Nation
> Revolution Revolution
> Kopulation Kopulation
>
> (p.136)

Coulmier is forced to ring the alarm bell and the stage direction indicates that he incites the nurses to employ extreme violence to bring the patients under control. Coulmier gives the signal for the curtain to be drawn on the proceedings. It was he who got the performance under way with his inroduction in the Prologue; it is he who now concludes the 'entertainment'. But the words that he used at the outset in the Prologue to the effect that patients no longer suffer in the old way because of the more enlightened, modern approach to treatment (p.12) now appear to have a hollow ring to them as in the Epilogue *Coulmier feuert die Pfleger zur äußersten Gewalt an* (p.136), as the only way to restore order. Words that have tripped off Coulmier's tongue earlier in the play: 'Erbauung', 'aufgeklärt', 'Bildung', 'Kunst', 'Menschenrechte', 'Vernunft' have by now somewhat lost their lustre. For the same methods — the resorting to physical violence — employed in the name of the Revolution and frowned upon by Coulmier when espoused by the likes of Marat and

Roux, are ultimately relied upon in a more modified form by Coulmier himself. In the end force is met with force, not enlightenment, and Coulmier's decision to draw a veil over events on stage is done out of desperation (*verzweifelt*) on his part. That one word 'verzweifelt' demonstrates fully that Coulmier feels threatened by the forces unleashed on stage in the shape of the eruptive behaviour of the volatile patients. (By this juncture Sade has deliberately abandoned control of his play.) In short, Weiss is ultimately reflecting a rather negative view of life through emphasis on death and anarchy. He may well have wished Marat to emerge victorious. But on this occasion the Revolution claims its own, just as the Revolution was in turn to be superseded by the Napoleonic empire. The successful revolution had still to materialize!

At the same time we should not be misled by that culminating stage direction: *Sade steht hoch auf seinem Stuhl und lacht triumphierend*. Despite deliberately ignoring Coulmier's repeated warning behests throughout the play and his laugh of triumph at the play's conclusion, Sade is in no way the victor. He may be seen as a victor over Marat in the sense that Marat is but a character written into the play which Sade is producing for the inmates at Charenton (though Weiss is at pains to 'authenticate' his Marat figure, as he indicates in the 'Anmerkungen zum geschichlichen Hintergrund unseres Stückes': 'Wenn es unsere Erfindung ist, ihn [Sade] Marat in dessen letzter Stunde gegenüberzustellen, so entspricht die geschilderte Lage Marats der Wirklichkeit...Die Äußerungen Marats im Lauf der Handlung entsprechen ihrem Inhalt nach, oft fast wortgetreu, seinen hinterlassenen Schriften', p.142). But he is decidedly not the victor over Coulmier, as we have indicated earlier.

Censorship, authority, discipline then are displayed — even if precariously — by Coulmier in the name of the Emperor. Not for nothing does he adopt a Napoleonic pose. His very being symbolizes the betrayal of the Revolution by the actuality of the Napoleonic Empire. That fact plus his 'role' as on-stage audience, demarcating the time-space markers and merging with the off-stage audience (yet at the same time helping to emphasize the stage illusion by the very

fact of being the on-stage audience), help to make the figure of
Coulmier into an important subsidiary character.

6. Putting on the Style

Simply put, *Marat/Sade* stands out in post-war drama for the totality of its effect, not for one outstanding character, one highlighted dramatic factor. Indeed if we were to isolate the central feature of this play — the debate of Marat and Sade — we might be forgiven for suspecting that Weiss had with that alone provided rather short measure; for the two characters are so entrenched in their thinking that neither seems vaguely near to persuading the other to change his respective stance. Sade had, of course, been initially in favour of the Revolution, had supported its aims for a time, only to grow tired and move away from its excesses — excesses stimulated by Marat's pamphlets and addresses to the nation. In that sense Sade had advanced his position, but that occurred *before* the 'staging' of his play in 1808. On stage therefore he is and remains a static character, a standpoint. Nor, in the play, will Marat change his stance. He has helped to foment the Revolution with his radical beliefs. Aware that the Revolution has not proceeded as he had wished, he has his doubts, but he will not change. And though Marat is granted by Sade a moment's pause on stage before his death to see into the future, he merely reaffirms his original position in the Epilogue. Marat and Sade, then, merely engage in debate that airs the problems, but certainly does not set out to solve them; they fail to engage in a polemic that reaches a proper climax and no real dramatic conclusion arises out of this philosophical debate, the more obviously so when we remember that in any case the two of them are essentially placed on different structural levels within the play. The rationality — the reasonableness — of their debate then has to be set against the unreason manifested in the theatrical context — the volatile behaviour of the patients that mirrors the anarchy in historical France at the time of the Revolution.

At the same time, the one dramatic event in the play — the assassination of Marat, which fittingly occurs almost at the end of the play — does not constitute in itself the key element, rather a byplay. The fact that the event too is made to drag over many scenes through repetition and interruption tends necessarily to deflect from the dramatic energy that should be inherent in such a situation.

It might be argued therefore that each of the two above ingredients — the act of murder and the philosophical argument — is in itself insufficient. But when taken together and — more important — when taken together with the subsidiary characters and the supporting roles they play in the proceedings and mixed in with a profusion of other elements (structural levels, music and mime, the imagery), we begin to recognize in their interaction before us a highly vibrant and colourful kaleidoscopic piece of theatre, to find an intricately woven tapestry that demands our full attention. It is this masterly, overt pretence, this theatricality — the very exaggeration of the elements — that helps to emphasize the descriptive *and* the critical vision of the situation.

We have referred earlier to the title of the play. It certainly caused Hans Werner Richter some misgivings: 'Es war ein langer, langatmiger und nach meiner Ansicht ganz unzeitgemäßer Titel, er belustigte mich auch, er hörte sich sehr nach einem Dramentitel längst vergangener Zeiten an' (*37*, p.262). It also provoked reaction when Weiss announced the title at his reading from *Marat* at the Gruppe 47 meeting at Saulgau (*37*, p.263). Did Weiss seek deliberately to make the title redolent of the past, perhaps quasi-intellectual, undramatic? Peter Brook, the director of the London production, takes a more basic view in his introduction to the published English translation (*3*):

> Starting with its title, everything about this play is designed to crack the spectator on the jaw, then douse him with ice-cold water, then force him to assess intelligently what has happened to him, then give him a kick in the balls, then bring him back to his senses again.

> It's not exactly Brecht and it's not Shakespeare either but
> it's very Elizabethan and very much of our time.

> It is also certainly reminiscent of Antonin Artaud's advocacy[7]
> — and an aggressive approach it is — to

> create a theatre in which violent physical images crush
> and hypnotise the sensibility of the spectator seized by
> the theatre as by a whirlwind of higher forces.

Weiss is only too aware of this himself, as he makes clear in the *Materialienbuch* (*14*, p.92) when he stresses the need for strong emotional effects that could only be achieved by Artaud's thesis.

Weiss's play is a far remove from the concern of the Naturalists that the theatre must minimize its 'theatricality'. Not exactly Brecht, says Brook. But we remember Brecht's insistence that the theatre stop pretending *not* to be a theatre, that it make undisguised use of song, dance, orchestra, lights, narrators, placards, slides. The 'theatricality' marks the divisions between the on-stage and off-stage worlds but at the same time Brecht's famed alienation technique is designed, in the words of Austin Quigley, to 'force the audience into a recognition of similarity in the context of difference.'[8] Brecht's technique aims therefore, Quigley argues, to make the audience react to his provisional theatrical world by recognizing its own world as similarly provisional. Alienation and yet connection. Among his favourite Brecht plays, incidentally, Weiss names *The Threepenny Opera* and *Mahagonny*. And we remember too Weiss on record as to the influence of Brecht on him as a dramatist: 'I learnt most from Brecht. I learnt clarity from him, the necessity of making clear the social question in a play. I learnt from his lightness. He is never heavy in the psychological German

---

[7]*The Theater and its Double*, tr. Mary Caroline Richards, New York, 1958, pp.82-83.
[8]*The Modern Stage and Other Worlds*, London: Methuen, 1985, p.31.

way' (*36*). Weiss spoke these words immediately before the London première of *Marat/Sade*, *not* in his days as a documentary dramatist of the later sixties! Weiss also admired Wedekind, whilst Strindberg, himself so influential for German Expressionism, influenced Weiss deeply too, especially with his later techniques and in the portrayal of a mad world and the insanity of life in the *Ghost Sonata* and *Inferno*. We are reminded of Weiss's essay on Strindberg, 'Gegen die Gesetze der Normalität' (*Akzente* 4, 1962), and of his translations of *Miss Julia* (in 1960) and *A Dream Play* (1963). Indeed Strindberg's words in *Preface to A Dream Play* have more than a passing relevance for Weiss:

> The author has tried to imitate the disconnected but seeming logical form of the dream. Anything may happen; everything is possible and probable. Time and space do not exist. On an insignificant background of reality, imagination designs and embroiders novel patterns: a medley of memories, experiences, free fancies, absurdities and improvisations.

The above is undoubtedly of pertinence to a Weiss play such as *Die Versicherung*, but is equally not out of place when we consider *Marat/Sade*, particularly bearing in mind the originally conceived form, the *Hörspiel*, still valid when the dream in this instance of the revolutionary ideal is fast becoming in fact a nightmare of terror.

Alienation and Involvement

Differing kinds of realism and theatricality then are observable in *Marat/Sade*. Weiss's fertile imagination produces, on the one hand, a magnificent sense of the absurd and the grotesque, and simultaneously, on the other, a parable — all set against a historical backcloth. The bath-house at Charenton, we know, serves as the setting for several locations in the inner play — the National

Assembly, the streets of Paris, with Marat's bath functioning also as his house, the tribune at the National Assembly, as well as symbolizing Marat's isolation (just as later Weiss heroes are to be isolated: Trotsky captive at his table in *Trotzki im Exil*, Hölderlin in his tower in *Hölderlin*), just as the asylum itself symbolizes Sade's isolation from the world. There is no change of scenery as such on stage and the audience is very much aware of the bath-house cubicles (that also serve as cells for the inmates) to the rear of the stage. The audience is also conscious of the fact that not only the patients who play the character roles — a paranoiac for Marat, a somnambulist for Corday, an erotomaniac for Duperret — catch the eye in any case because of their various disorders, but that the bulk of the other patients also present on stage as extras for mimes, chorus and voices, are similarly afflicted. Further, we are informed (p.12), any not required devote themselves to their autistic exercises. In short, their very presence sets the atmosphere behind the acting area. Weiss's dramatic purpose is to provoke the spectator emotionally as well as to instil a didactic interest in his play. We are forcefully reminded of the fact that this is a stage (even if the stage has its own reality), and our critical awareness is heightened. The audience witnesses therefore the intellectual debate between Marat and Sade with its measured, orderly tones against the background of the mad world of the asylum. Weiss neatly identifies, though, through the subject of that debate, the mad world of revolutionary France with the goings-on in the asylum. Roux in particular (though not exclusively) succeeds quickly through his rabble-rousing addresses to the people in agitating the patients to the point where the latter get out of control and need restraining by the nurses. Charenton is testimony to the existence of madness in the world. The fact that the play is about the Revolution itself and man's political madness heightens the case Weiss is making. Horizons merge, for the very structure of Weiss's play with its three levels of time and space both delineate and break the boundaries. Whole scenes or part of a scene, one character or a combination of characters exemplify the alienatory factor designed to mirror 'similarity in the context of difference'. To state merely the most obvious instances: the opening and concluding scenes.

Coulmier's words in the Prologue set out a declaration of intent; the Epilogue sums up the foregoing happenings. No sooner has Marat been assassinated by Corday than the Herald bids him step forth from his bath to recapitulate with the other characters their respective positions. Between that formal framework for the play we encounter examples of alienation in every scene in some form, either in the spoken word or indicated in the stage directions as deed or gesture, examples almost too numerous to individualize. We think of Roux, Corday, Marat, Coulmier, Sade, the Herald in turn actually interrupting the action of the play or looking directly at, even directly addressing the off-stage audience. We have already dwelt on the first five names. But the Herald too fulfils a notably significant function in that he acts as intermediary to the 'actors' and the audiences on and off stage. He is there as a constant reminder that it is all but a piece of theatre: by introducing the characters to us in the Presentation, pointing out that the various roles are just roles being filled by inmates for the performance; by 'setting' the scenes, informing us as to what is going on; operating as prompter when characters forget their lines (see, for example, Scenes 15, 17, 23) and cueing characters to appear (in Scenes 7, 29); and — arguably most important — by seeking to put, and keep, in perspective everything that is happening on stage. He it is who interrupts Coulmier's appeal in Scene 11 and encourages the continuation of the scene by pointing out the temporal distinction between 1793 and 1808 (pp.33f.), and similarly in Scene 13 which he concludes by mocking Coulmier's immediately preceding words on the goodness and understanding of the Church, the irony here heightened by the Herald's accompanying gesture:

> Sollte jemand im Publikum sich getroffen fühlen
> so bitten wir denselben seinen Ärger abzukühlen
> und in Freundlichkeit zu bedenken
> daß wir den Blick hier in die Vergangenheit lenken
> in der alles anders war als heute

Heute sind wir natürlich gottesfürchtige Leute
schlägt ein Kreuzzeichen
(pp.42f.)

The Herald is on hand likewise to conclude Scenes 14, 16 and 24
with further appeals to the off-stage audience as well as the on-stage
audience to recognize the differences between the past and the
present and not to confuse the issues. He similarly brings the first act
to a close and gets the second under way. He it is who informs the
audience of Sade's dramatic intention in Scene 31 and who invites
the characters to recapitulate their cases in the Epilogue.

His job then is to keep the flow of the play going, to sustain
the illusion, at the same time undertaking the linking of the inner and
the outer times and actions; to draw distinctions, yet also the threads
of allusion. Co-ordinator, commentator, but not the ultimate
controller of the events on stage (for at the end in the Epilogue he
too as one of the inmates succumbs to the frenzied mood that has
erupted and it is Coulmier who draws a veil over proceedings by
ordering the curtain to be drawn).

The Song and Dance and Mime Routine

Let us remember too that Weiss was very interested in the
sixties in reviving the popular forms of entertainment. Consider here
some of Weiss's comments contained in his note 'Zur Inszenierung
von "Nacht mit Gästen"', 1963 (*4*, p.262):

Vom Kasper-Spiel wäre hier das Grobschlächtige,
Possenhafte zu entnehmen, die starken Effekte, das laut
Herausgerufene, oft falsch Betonte, das Aggressive und
Grauenhafte unter der scheinbaren Lustigkeit...Die
starken Farben, gern bis Grellheit...der stark vereinfachte
Dekor, der nur die absolut notwendigen Gegenstände
enthält, sowie die stilisierte Gestik — dies alles ähnelt

einander in den beiden Theaterformen (Kasper-Spiel und Kabuki-Theater)...Sehr wichtig ist die Musikbegleitung.

All of the above is applicable to *Marat/Sade* (as indeed it could be said of certain other of Weiss's plays: for example, *Gesang vom Lusitanischen Popanz*). The musical accompaniment takes several forms in the play. There are five musicians, themselves inmates of the asylum. They play harmonium, lute, flute, trumpet and drums. At the start in Scene 3 they play ceremonious music as the actors assume their places. And soft ceremonious music introduces the Epilogue, but following Coulmier's words of hope for the future in the Napoleonic Empire the tempo changes and the orchestra starts to play the final march; the music gets louder (*Die Musik steigert sich*) and a change of mood occurs as the music increases in intensity to echo the increasing frenzy of the patients as they get out of control (*Musik und Marschtakt werden immer gewaltsamer...Mit dröhnendem Marschtakt...Musik, Geschrei und Trampeln wächst zum Sturm an*, pp.135f.). The processional music which should have been triumphal to celebrate the successful Napoleonic times (and visually a banner of Napoleon is symbolically let down) becomes discordant as tumultuous disorder reigns — essentially so, to sound the insanity of the world.

A military march had been the tempo shortly before for the musical revue that comprises Scene 31, and there it is sustained — without interruption — as the Four Singers sing the course of history from 1793 to 1808. An entirely different rhythmic beat had been heard, however, in Scene 10. Here the music served to underscore the monotonous rhythm of the dance of death performed by the patients as victims went to their death at the guillotine, the execution announced by a long drumroll (p.30). (Three drumrolls beat out similarly, incidentally, in Scene 28, in anticipation of Marat's forthcoming execution at the hands of Corday, p.113). When Sade points out to Marat (on the occasion of Corday's second visit in Scene 25) the sufferings of the people and their dissatisfaction at the course of events, the music adopts a suitable (and ironic) tragic tone (*Die Musik geht zu einem tragischen Anklang über*, p.84). At the close of that same scene Marat is left with his thoughts which lead, in the following scene, to the physical presentation on stage of nightmare situations from his past. In anticipation of that, the music changes mood too (*Die Musik geht in ein dramatisches Grollen über*, p.85). Nor do our ears fail to pick out the increasingly familiar Corday-theme, which is played as a leitmotif throughout the play when she makes her appearance.

In addition to the instrumental music, the voice is heard to good effect. We think perhaps first of the Four Singers. For their part, they can be seen immediately as part of the tradition of the *Jahrmarktsbuden* (p.16), just as the Herald is meant so to be identified through his dress (*trägt über dem Anstaltshemd einen Harlekinkittel*, p.9). They are singers, comedians and also act as representatives of the people. In that last capacity they reflect the changing mood of the people through the shifts of fortune of the Revolution. They perform the recitative in the homage to Marat in Scene 5, whilst the Chorus adds its voice in the background, before they join forces to sing a refrain that expresses the sense of frustration felt by the people:

> Marat was ist aus unserer Revolution geworden
> Marat wir wolln nicht mehr warten bis morgen
> Marat wir sind immer noch arme Leute
> und die versprochenen Änderungen wollen wir heute
>
> (p.21)

This same united rumbling discontent is voiced twice more — but with a small yet significant change of word in the last line on each occasion, a change that marks a development in the progression of the mob's feelings. In the first instance above, the changes that they want now are the ones that were originally promised ('versprochen') by the leaders of the Revolution; on the next occasion (in Scene 16), the reaction demonstrates that patience is running thin — now the changes are ones that are deemed necessary ('notwendig'); the third time, the situation has become critical — the changes referred to here (Scene 26) are ones demanded ('gefordert'). We shall have cause to return to the Four Singers shortly.

If the Four Singers have indulged in the operatic recitative on occasion (and as Sade himself does in Scene 30), then further quasi-operatic offerings are forthcoming in scenes involving Corday and Duperret. In Scene 17 where the two conduct their first conversation, each addresses the other *im Stil einer Arie*; *im gleichen Arienstil, doch mit Feuer*; *leidenschaftlich, im Arienstil wie zuvor* (pp.52-54). Again, when looking forward to the vision of social and political harmony in the course of their second conversation, they resort to the same form of the aria (*im Arienstil*; *im Arienstil singend*, p.77). Given the circumstances of the nobility of sentiment being expressed to the accompaniment of Duperret's sexual advances to Corday, the scene even assumes the overtones of a Mozartian comic opera. Yet at the same time that very mode in the theatrical context also suggests a criticism of traditional opera, produces a note of alienation as disillusioning in its way as the dance of death in Scene 10, the discordant march music in the Epilogue, and many another musical example in the course of the play.

We should not ignore further variations of vocal offerings. Consider the discordant sound of laughter, whistling, booing — the stage directions make frequent reference in the play to *schrilles Gelächter*; *schrille Pfiffe*; *schrill grölend; Pfiffe und Getrampel*; *Geschrei der Empörung*; *Buh-Rufe*; *Aufruhr und Geschrei*. And by way of contrast, the tranquillizing litany of the sisters calms the upset patients (in Scene 6). Their litanies can also be heard in Scene 13 during Marat's liturgy when he is accompanied by the chorus of patients, just as their prayers had been uttered in Scene 11. And the variety of sound is extended through the very variety of address — from the literary, intellectual style of Sade and Marat, Voltaire and Lavoisier, to the doggerel of the Herald, the sing-song of Corday to the coarseness of the inmates. All contribute towards the dazzling, contrasting combinations.

So often the music is combined too with mime and dance. The first obvious illustration of this occurs in Scene 10, 'Lied und

Pantomime von Cordays Ankunft in Paris.' *Die Pantomime des Messerkaufs wird ausgeführt*, as the Four Singers sing of Corday's purchase of the dagger with which to murder Marat. With the sound and sight of the guillotine at work, the mime procession develops into a dance of death: *Der Pantomimenzug wird mächtiger und entwickelt sich zu einem Totentanz. Die Musik unterstreicht den eintönigen Rhythmus* (p.30). And as Marat addresses the audience in the following scene and speaks of Death's triumph at the guillotine, *Die Hinrichtung wird pantomimisch dargestellt* (p.32). Again, in Scene 13, as Marat delivers his liturgy, referred to above, a complementary mime is performed by the Four Singers depicting church dignitaries. The Four Singers perform a further mime and song in Scene 19 in which they illustrate Sade's words on the material values in life ('to him that hath shall be given'). And as Marat awaits the arrival of Corday that will spell his doom, they perform a slow *carmagnole*, the song and dance so popular in France at the time of the Revolution.

Arguably the most provocative mime in the play (even more than the execution scene in 'Triumph des Todes') is the copulation mime to accompany Sade's recitative on the need for copulation to go with the Revolution. The murder scene we shall refer to later.

The prominence given in *Marat/Sade* to the songs and music-hall routines leads us to the legitimate query whether such serve to conceal a lack of real action in the play, cause a lack of unifying dramatic tension, even actually *diminish* meaning. At least one critic believes these formalistic aspects act as a disadvantage *vis-à-vis* the 'political' utterances: 'Der formale Aufwand des Stücks macht das zur Nebensache, wofür er erfunden war' (*14*, p.136). The songs, the revue, the dance and mime routines are undoubtedly intended by Weiss to illustrate the text and its meaning as well as to produce disillusionment by means of their shock effect. Whatever their ultimate effect, they unquestionably highlight the notion and (when we witness a live performance) presence of the theatre and its traditional modes.

Stations of the Cross

Weiss's admiration for Strindberg, to which we have referred earlier, would have made him aware of the Swedish writer's play *To Damascus* which, like the *Ghost Sonata*, foreshadowed Expressionism. Indeed that work in particular served as an immediate model for the characteristic Expressionist *Stationendrama*, a type of play which presented a series of stages or tableaux showing the spiritual progress of an individual. Clearly it is analogous to the notion of the Stations of the Cross, but for the activists in the Expressionist period 'spiritual' was to be understood primarily in the context of social and political change. The 'religious' connotation is less than religiously applied. Such is the case here in *Marat/Sade*. The *Stationendrama* then suits Weiss's purpose excellently as he portrays Marat going to his death as a martyr of the Revolution in quasi-biblical terms with the allusion to Calvary (and the crown of thorns through the award to Marat of a crown of leaves in Scene 5; historically, on the day of his acquittal by the Revolutionary Tribunal, following an abortive attempt by the Girondins to convict him in April 1793, a woman had placed a crown of roses on Marat's brow). The Herald had, after all, spoken of Roux seeing himself as Marat's apostle, 'weil dieser wie ein Gekreuzigter ist' (p.62). (This religious tone is obviously further in evidence elsewhere, as, for example, in Marat's liturgy and the sisters' litanies and of course in the perverted prayer to Satan in Scene 14).

The stations in *Marat/Sade* follow each other as independent dramatic episodes. They are of course thematically linked by the Revolution and its effects, but not constantly dependent upon each other in terms of time or action for continuity. That notwithstanding, Weiss does achieve some nice balancing. Consider the build-up of mood in Scenes 5 to 8. In paying their homage to Marat, the people give the first hint of dissatisfaction at the close of Scene 5. The collective discontent gathers momentum in the next scene, though the mood of unrest is stifled. In the next scene, however, the specific (and historical) voice of opposition from an individual is raised, as

Corday announces her intention to free the people from the tyranny of Marat. *His* purpose is not to be gainsaid either, as he cries out in Scene 8 'Ich bin die Revolution', thereby ensuring his dramatic destiny, affirming his historical fate. Or again, we might think of the following sequence of scenes that illustrate reality and idealism in stark contrast: Scenes 19 and 20 comprise Roux's rabble-rousing exploits. He figuratively whips up the people into a frenzy as he tells them how they have been persecuted. In Scene 21 we have the spectacle of Sade actually being whipped by Corday who persecutes him — of course, at the latter's bidding — as he talks to Marat of the Revolution. Marat's own persecution is witnessed in Scene 22. On the other hand, the Herald shows the reverse of the coin in Scene 23, where he brings on Duperret and Corday for their second conversation.

Essentially, though, the technique of the *Stationendrama* permits Weiss to display his control over the pace of the play, where the practised eye of the painter, cineaste or dramatist surveys the scene before him. We forget the earlier careers of Weiss at our peril. The association of the world of the cinema and the theatre for Weiss has already been recorded by him in his 'Notiz zu "Die Versicherung".' The comment was written in 1968 in preparation for the play's first German staging in the spring of 1969 in Cologne: 'Die surrealistisch-visionäre Form des Dramas hängt eng zusammen mit meinen damaligen filmischen Versuchen' (*4*, p.260). The play itself of course goes back to 1952, completed shortly after his prose text *Der Schatten des Körpers des Kutschers*, where cinematographic techniques were also in evidence. The techniques of the cinema were to be found too in his later play *Trotzki im Exil* (1969), as Weiss readily admitted in interview: 'By means of an unrealistic arrangement of time Trotsky's career is critically illustrated, in flashbacks somewhat like in a film...I have endeavoured to present a perspective which leads to our present situation.'[9] In fact the words could easily and equally be applied to *Marat/Sade*. The same unrealistic arrangement of time critically illustrates in this case Marat's career. And certainly Weiss seeks to present to us a

---

[9]*The Times*, 21 June 1969.

perspective that leads to the present situation of the later twentieth century. So we find before us the flashback (and indeed flashforward) of time as well as the moment captured in a frame frozen before the camera rolls again. Weiss hereby switches the pace most effectively in a variety of ways. After the ceremonious opening to the play, the stifled unrest that threatens after Roux has started to agitate the people with his radicalism contrasts with the somnambulism of Corday in the following scene. She is then kept waiting before she makes her first visit to Marat because of the intervening Scene 8. That first visit is then followed by a flashback to her arrival in Paris from Caen, illustrated in the song and mime that comprises Scene 10. And Weiss incorporates in his play several other instances where the natural flow of events is deliberately halted: the debate between Marat and Sade is interrupted (for example, by the regrettable intervention of the patient that constitutes Scene 14); the flashback in Scene 26 when visions from Marat's past flash physically before his eyes on stage; conversely the flashforward in Scene 31 when the singers perform their musical revue of the years after 1793.

Also there are the tableaux where the silent and motionless groupings form a picturesque presentation. We think immediately of Scene 3: *Die gesamte Gruppe nimmt die Haltung eines heroischen Tableaus ein* (p.13). We recall Duperret and Corday in Scene 23: they have been talking of noble ideals, Corday is then led back by one of the sisters. *Corday wird zu einer heroischen Pose zurechtgestellt.* On finishing his lines, Duperret likewise assumes a suitable pose: *Auch Duperret nimmt eine dazu passende Pose ein, so daß sie ein angenehmes Schlußbild darstellen* (p.78). A picturesque presentation indeed, the moment framed. Or consider the opening of the second act where the meeting of the National Assembly awaits the sign from the Herald to get under way: *Er gibt dem Orchester ein Zeichen mit dem Stab. Ein Tusch. Die Umsitzenden im Tableau pfeifen, trampeln und scharren mit den Füßen* (p.99).

The most celebrated tableau is of course the murder scene. The Herald blows shrilly on his whistle at the end of Scene 30 to freeze the moment when Corday is about to plunge the dagger into Marat.

All the players, patients, nurses, sisters remain immobile in their positions whilst the Herald announces Sade's dramatic intent. After the completion of the ensuing musical revue, the Herald announces the murder. The deed is done in a moment, accompanied by a single scream from the patients. Action followed by the moment being frozen, a still from a series of film frames — or a painting, as David's famous picture of the assassination of Marat is reproduced on stage. The painter, himself a deputy, had in fact visited Marat on the 12th July, the day before the murder, and found the latter writing his thoughts for the safety of the people.[10] Jacques Louis David (born in 1748) was recognized as a late eighteenth-century neo-classical artist as well as the most talented delineator of the French Revolution before becoming the major exponent in paint of the pomp of Napoleonic Empire. A member of the extreme Jacobin group, he can be seen as a politically committed artist — he was called the Robespierre of the brush — and his revolutionary commitment at the time is best represented in his masterpiece *The Dead Marat* (*Le Marat assassiné*), completed shortly after the murder of the revolutionary leader in 1793. This *pietà* of the Revolution, with its own theatricality of presentation, clearly provides the inspiration for Scene 32 (which Weiss incidentally acknowledges in the stage directions at that point, p.82). Two years earlier, in 1791, David had painted another celebrated picture *The Oath of the Tennis Court* (*Le Serment du Jeu de Paume*). An entry in the *Notizbuch* relating to a visit to Paris by Weiss is informative:

> Der Ballsaal 'Jeu de Paume' von David (Vorbild für die Bühne zum Marat): diese phantastische Raumbildung — mit den offnen Fenstern links oben, den weit hineinwehenden Gardinen, die riesigen kahlen Wände, ringsum das Gestühl, die gedrängte stürmische Versammlung mit dem erhöht stehenden Sprecher in der Mitte. (*8*, p.390)

---

[10]Simon Schama, *Citizens*, Viking, 1989, p.731.

(Incidentally, we find also in that same *Notizbuch* (*8*, pp.502f.) a photograph of the corner house with the tower in the Rue de l'Ecole de Médecine in Paris where Marat lived, as well as a sketch plan drawn by Weiss of Marat's apartment in that house, including the room with the bath; further, there are pictures of Damiens, Marat's death, Sade in prison, a guillotine, a torture scene, an illustration of hydrotherapy to be found in the *Notizbücher* (*7*, pp.202-05, 208).

Ritual

It is patently clear then to spectator and reader alike right at the outset that Weiss is at considerable pains to emphasize a sense of ritual in *Marat/Sade*. Indeed we encounter it everywhere, not just in the opening scenes (Assembly, Prologue, Preparation and Presentation). For immediately the inner play commences we find the ritual of the homage to Marat: *Die vier Sänger und andere Patienten stellen sich zu einer Apotheose um die Wanne auf; Die Patienten im Zug vollführen einstudierte Gebärden der Huldigung; Marat wird feierlich in die Wanne zurückgesetzt* (pp.19-21). Patently ritualistic are the very exchanges between Marat and Sade. Constant ritual surrounds the performance of Corday, not least in the elaborate preparations by the sisters to get her ready (*Dies gleicht einer Ritualhandlung*, p.24) and the repetitive playing of the Corday theme by the orchestra. There is a ritual in Simonne attending Marat in his bath. The *Totentanz* and the *Hinrichtung* contain ritualistic elements. And what of Marat's liturgy and the sisters' litanies; even the meeting of the National Assembly where the chorus is divided into sections to reflect the factional sympathies? Further, we might consider the ritual in the behavioural patterns of the patients themselves, the murder scene, the 'copulation/revolution' ritual.

Linked with Corday is the ritual of copulation — symbol of animal violence — that can be seen in three stages: the foreplay with Sade under the whip; the climax in the murder of Marat; the interruptus (Scene 31) where the historical revue of events is performed. Indeed the most persistent form of ritual in *Marat/Sade* is arguably to be detected in Weiss's seeming penchant for certain numbers. We cannot help but be made aware of his preoccupation with the numerals three and eleven, either singly or in combination. We note that *Marat/Sade* has thirty-three scenes and we recall that at the time of working on *Marat/Sade*, Weiss was also interested in Dante's *Inferno*. He was busy with his *Vorübung zum dreiteiligen Drama divina commedia* (it was first to appear in *Akzente* 4, 1965); his interest is further manifested in *Gespräch über Dante* (in *Merkur* 6, 1965). Those two pieces of writing provide a link between *Marat/Sade* and *Die Ermittlung*, where we find eleven cantos, each divided into three parts. (The figure eleven was subsequently incorporated by Weiss into *Gesang vom Lusitanischen Popanz*, *Mockinpott* and *Vietnam Diskurs*). Here in *Marat/Sade* the threes abound. We have spoken elsewhere of the three levels of time and space structures. Also very obvious is the threefold visit of Corday to the house of Marat that fateful day. Her arrival at the door on each occasion is announced by the Herald knocking three times with his staff on the floor (in Scenes 9, 25 and 30). He has also knocked three times when Corday was presented in Scene 7, just as he had done likewise for the general Presentation in Scene 4. A loud knocking is heard three times for the preparation for Corday's third visit and three drum rolls too in that same Scene 28. We think of the division of the chorus into three sections at the meeting of the National Assembly. Threefold verbal utterances occur too as in the repetition of the phrase 'Denn was wäre schon diese Revolution/ohne eine allgemeine Kopulation' (Scene 30); the threefold repetition by the Four Singers and Chorus of the refrain 'Marat was ist uns aus unsrer Revolution geworden' (Scenes 5, 16 and 26); even the stuttering of the teacher in Scene 26 comes in threes! In the context of the play *Marat/Sade*, dealing as it does with the theme of the Revolution and its effects, the insistence on threes might seem ironically to breathe the spirit of the time with *its* threefold aim of *Liberté, Egalité, Fraternité!*

Ritual then forms an integral part of the multitude of devices that Weiss has plainly introduced into his play to ensure a colossal kaleidoscopic theatricality. It is his intention to present to the playgoer a ritual of formal performance to illustrate the sense of order. It is but an illusion, an overt pretence. For, in his pursuance of patterns of opposites, Weiss is really showing us through the events portrayed on stage the reverse of the coin. The notion of regularity suggested, for example, in the patterns of litany, liturgy, march, tableau gives way before the onset of unreason, violence and anarchy, and the play ends in discord. And the variety of moods he produces — from triumph to disaster, harmony to disorder, from the serious to the absurd, the ceremonious to the grotesque — the dramatist quickly and deliberately interchanges to jell with or jar the scenic presentation at a given moment.

7. Reactions and Relationships

Weiss's own response to the West Berlin première of *Marat/Sade* is recorded, with feeling, in an entry in his *Notizbuch*:

> Die magischen Handlungen vor Beginn der Vorstellung.
> Die Beschwörungen, das Über-die-Schulter-Spucken,
> das Verteilen von Amuletten
>
> Grass in der Pause böse an mir vorbei
> Nahm mir das Stück übel
>
> Von den 'Kollegen': keiner —
> gestützt hatten mich: Hans Mayer, Swinarski, Karlheinz
> Braun, Gunilla —   (7, p.237)

That same night is recalled by Hans Werner Richter:

> Es gab Beifall, doch schon in der Pause spürte man
> wieder die Ablehnung, die sich auch schon in Saulgau
> bemerkbar gemacht hatte. Uwe Johnson saß einige
> Stuhlreihen vor mir und las scheinbar gelangweilt die
> Zeitung, und Günter Grass verhielt sich nicht viel
> anders. Es kam mir wie eine demonstrative
> Nichtanerkennung vor. Zum Schluß gab es viel Beifall
> von den Rängen, aber nur vereinzelt im Parkett...
>
> Die Premierenfeier fand in einem Restaurant, nur wenige
> Schritte vom Schillertheater entfernt, statt... Als er
> endlich kam, gratulierte ich ihm, blieb aber mit meiner
> Gratulation fast allein. Weder Günter Grass noch Uwe

Johnson schlossen sich an, noch die anderen. Eine Front
der Ablehnung tat sich auf. Sie standen alle herum,
diskutierten miteinander, schwiegen aber sofort, wenn
Peter in die Nähe kam. Die meisten von ihnen waren
offensichtlich enttäuscht oder hatten etwas anderes
erwartet. Keiner sprach eine Anerkennung oder ein Lob
aus. Ärger stieg in Peter auf...am liebsten hätte er seine
Wut herausgeschrien...er hatte Beifall erwartet und fand
nur stumme Verweigerung. Der ganze Premierenabend
konnte jeden Moment explodieren, ja, der große Krach,
den ich in der Gruppe 47 so lange verhindert hatte,
konnte ausgerechnet hier auf dieser Premierenfeier
ausbrechen und vieles zerstören...immerhin kam es nicht
zu einem völligen Desaster. Die schlechte Stimmung
ließ sich nicht in eine andere, bessere verändern, und
Peter blieb gekränkt, den ganzen Abend über.
                                                    (*37*, pp.265f.)

It sounds like a disaster, but in fact the above passage reveals more
about the attitudes and position of the Gruppe 47 itself at that time
than it does about Peter Weiss and the fate of his play. As Richter
indicates here and elsewhere, the Gruppe 47 was already beginning
to fall apart through internal factional feuding among the writers
both on literary and political grounds. Weiss records the atmosphere
he encountered at his first meeting of the group he attended in 1962
at Wannsee, Berlin: 'Ich geriet in eine Versammlung, in der es
schwirrte von Rankünen, Eifersüchten, Rivalitäten, Machtkämpfen,
Kulturpolik' (*8*, p.730).

But there was no doubting the general enthusiastic approval of
Marat/Sade from other quarters. Henning Rischbieter could write of
that same opening performance: 'Der Erfolg war stürmisch. Die
Mehrheit des Publikum erwärmte sich am Beifall; Autor und
Regisseur wurden mit Bravorufen überschüttet. Wenige Buhs gingen
im langanhaltenden Applaus unter.'[11] And of the piece itself, the
review continued: 'Wir haben seit Brecht und seinem Theater ein

---

[11]*Theater heute*, 1964/6, p.21.

Werk von diesem Ausdruckswillen nicht mehr gehabt.' The *Times* thought the play at its London première 'the most ambitious example of the Theatre of Cruelty yet to appear. Practically every influence in operation in intellectual high fashion is to be found in this play.'[12] In later comment by British critics, Colin Innes considered *Marat/Sade* to be, due to its complexity, one of the most electrifying experiences on the post-war stage, 'the best known and most successful example of dialectical theatre.'[13] Critics too touch on the politics as well as the aesthetics of the play. August Closs saw that

> this gruesome display of mental derangement has as its
> background a highly topical theme: individualism (de
> Sade) against collectivism (Marat), *or* West versus East,
> the decadence of extreme egoism against the fanatical
> puritanism of the revolutionary. Parallels between the
> 1810s and the 1960s, Napoleon's regime and West
> German 'Restauration' are evident.[14]

Brigitte Thurm argued: 'Bei Weiss wird das Hospiz von Charenton zum Gleichnis des bürgerlichen Staates im allgemeinen und dem der Bundesrepublik im besonderen.'[15]

What we are surely finding evidence of here are varying reactions of critics to different stagings of the piece. After all, as the *Great Soviet Encyclopedia*[16] points out, 'the duality of meaning in the play provided the grounds for its various stage interpretations in different countries.' The West Berlin production by Swinarski was seen as a superb example of Brechtian dialectical theatre. To that end Swinarski had basically cut the Epilogue and even drawn the curtain between the patients and Marat and Sade in debate to allow for no possible distraction from that unhindered, open-ended dialogue. Yet

---

[12]*The Times*, 21 August 1964, p.11.
[13]Innes, op. cit., p.197.
[14]*Twentieth Century German Literature*, ed. A. Closs, Cressett, 1969, p.101.
[15]'Gesellschaftliche Relevanz und künstlerische Subjektivität' in *Weimarer Beiträge* 15 (1969), 1091-1102. Here 1093.
[16]Macmillan, 1974, Vol. IV, p.689.

the East German writer Stephan Hermlin was to look critically at precisely this 'scheinbare Unentschiedenheit des Ausgangs',[17] and indeed members of the Berliner Ensemble who attended the Swinarski performance complained at what they considered the right-wing values of the play.

Weiss himself makes reference to the attitude of the Berliner Ensemble in an entry in the *Notizbuch* dated 26 March 1965, as well as to his own feelings on witnessing Hanns Anselm Perten's staging of his piece for the Rostock theatre:

> Für das BE war der Marat ein *konterrevolutionäres* Stück. Weigel wies es ab. Perten aber hatte die Aufführung durchgekämpft. Allein das schon eine Leistung. Auf seiner Bühne: ein *revolutionäres* Stück. Wurde plötzlich auch Lehrstück für mich: wie Marats Stimme durchdringt auch dort, wo ich geglaubt hatte, er müße aufgeben. (7, p.354)

In Rostock there was no question of an equal, open-ended debate. Here were clear-cut ideological groupings where Marat was portrayed as the orthodox Marxist and Sade comes a very poor second as (in Weiss's words, *14*, pp.101ff.) 'Der Dekadente, der Libertin und Lebensuntüchtige.' The patients form now a disciplined organized proletariat whose expressions of protest — far from insane — are voiced against social injustices imposed by the repressive establishment (symbolized by the authoritarianism of the Napoleonic Coulmier and the use of straitjackets in Charenton).

Now undoubtedly Weiss did feel at heart that Marat was the true hero, 'der Revolutionär, der die Gesellschaftsordnung, heute also die bürgerliche, verändern will.' As he said in an interview at the time of the East German staging: 'Ich habe immer wieder betont, daß ich das Prinzip Marats als das richtige und überlegene ansehe. Eine Inszenierung meines Stückes, in der am Ende nicht Marat als der moralische Sieger erscheint, wäre verfehlt.'[18] At the same time it did

---

[17]*Deutschlandsender*, Berlin, 17 December 1964.
[18]*Demokrat*, Berlin, 3 March 1965.

not prevent Weiss from voicing a concern over Perten's production in an interview with A. Alvarez (*32*), in which he felt that the effect of the dialectical oppositions would have been stronger if Marat's victory had been presented in a more complex manner.

Weiss had already had his reservations over the London production by Peter Brook. At the Aldwych Theatre, Brook had placed the patients in the foreground of the action, not regarding them as merely part of the scenery as Swinarski had arguably tended to do, and certainly not organizing them in the way that Perten was to perceive. They were highly individualized and the image of the madhouse world became a dominant one, where the intellectual, dialectical force of the debate was incorporated into the general atmosphere of Charenton. With Brook, as against Swinarski, a stronger and more dangerous madness prevailed in the asylum. Weiss did not complain officially at the time, though it was known that he was less than fully satisfied with the production — the more understandably so when Weiss was apparently stating his views emphatically enough on the play in an interview with *The Times* (*36*) immediately before the London première, where he is reported as saying that 'it is a Marxist play. Marat should be the victor: if de Sade wins the debate, that is bad' and adding that Napoleon represents Stalinism which lies on the other side of Marat and de Sade sees it.' The political ambivalence of Brook's production would not have made *that* obvious to the spectators! The Stockholm production of *Marat/Sade* incidentally also had its attendant problems for Peter Weiss. Whilst respecting Ingmar Bergman's production, he was undoubtedly at variance with the Swede's primary interest in the psychology of the characters involved.

In short, therefore, Weiss found himself, not for the first nor the last time in his career, on the proverbial horns of a dilemma. Simply put, he was facing the age-old problem of the function of the artist. His relationships with directors and producers were seemingly rarely straightforward, indeed proved on occasion very problematical. He draws attention to the general problem in the *Notizbuch*:

> Die Funktion des Dramatikers ist von subalterner
>   Art
> die Macht wird ausgeübt von den Regisseuren
> die Institutions-Theater verkörpern
>   Feudal-Herrschaft
>   (8, p.422)

Again, in a letter to the *Frankfurter Allgemeine Zeitung* (8 October 1976) on the subject of 'Der Autor als Ware' (8, p.529), he writes of how 'In der Theaterinstitution, diesem kleinen Abbild der Klassengesellschaft, gehört der Stückesschreiber zu den Lohnarbeitern.' He comments bitterly on the 'Regisseurtheater' in the West:

> Vom Regisseur hängt es ab, welche Schlagkraft, welches Anziehungsvermögen, welche Überraschungseffekte aus der Rohware herauszuziehen sind. Durch die geltenden Produktionsverhältnisse hat sich der Regisseur zu dieser Rolle verleiten lassen. Für ihn geht es darum, soviel Originalität, Genialität, Schockwirkungen wie nur irgend möglich an den Tag zu legen, um seine eigne Stellung in der Unterhaltungsindustrie zu konsolidieren oder, besser noch, zu steigern. Das Regisseurtheater ist die direkte Folge des rasend hochgetriebenen Kommerzialismus.

In such circumstances the ultimate verdict on the play that is being staged can well be determined more by the director than the author himself. The London theatre-goers attending the Aldwych Theatre performance of *Marat/Sade*, for example, might pertinently have been asked at the time which of the two Peters, Brook or Weiss, had succeeded in impressing and influencing them the more. Weiss records more favourable impressions of the theatre tradition in the German Democratic Republic in his *Notizbuch*:

> Die Theatertradition, die es in der DDR noch gibt — die enge Zusammenarbeit zw. Autor u Regisseur — nicht

wie im Westen, wo Regisseur den Text höchstens als
Ausgangspunkt benutzt, um sich selber zur Geltung zu
bringen. DDR Theater, wie ich es bei Perten erlebte, der
den Text analysiert und dabei die Inhalte herausschält —
auch aufmerksam macht auf Fehler, die schöpferische
Arbeit des Regisseurs dort, Kunst u Wissenschaft zu
verbinden. Im Westen nur das Hervortreiben des
Genialischen, mit allen Mitteln. (*8*, pp.638f.)

We might remember of course that despite his approval for the
practice described above, Weiss had carped somewhat at Perten's
rather simplistic portrayal of Sade. And even if Perten did basically
serve Weiss well in his production of *Marat/Sade* (as indeed in his
later productions of *Hölderlin* and *Der Prozeß*), the very system in
the shape of the cultural functionaries in the DDR imposed its own
difficulties. Weiss makes that very evident through his frank
admission of the requirements demanded of him for the eventual
staging of *Marat/Sade*. Weiss talks of the counter-revolutionary
tendencies of Sade, 'die in den Vorbesprechungen über eine
eventuelle Aufführung stark kritisiert wurden' (*14*, pp.112f.). Making
Marat the positive hero was the only sure way of ensuring the
staging. 'Es schien dies, da das Stück starke Schwierigkeiten hatte, in
der DDR überhaupt zur Aufführung zu kommen, der einzige Weg
zur bühnenmäßigen Verwirklichung.'

Hardly surprising then is the fact that Weiss seems almost
pointedly not to signal any crystal-clear rejection or endorsement of
different stagings of *Marat/Sade*. The sheer precariousness of his
balance on the politico-theatrical high wire perhaps partly dictates
and explains his ambivalent stance at a given time. He can tell *The
Times* in August 1964, for example, that *Marat/Sade* is a Marxist
play, whilst saying to A. Alvarez even in the November of the same
year in a BBC interview that 'I stand in the middle. I represent the
third standpoint which doesn't please me.' In 1965 he is on record in
print admitting to Alvarez (*32*): 'The only alternative is that I give
my doubts, that I show my situation of doubtfulness and the great
difficulties I undergo to find some way out of it. That is the only

thing I can reach.' He is still talking in this vein with Alvarez (again) at the time of the New York production in 1965.[19] The same Weiss in the interim has been speaking of *Marat/Sade* as a topical political play about current society, singing his praises of Marat and arguing that one should not write other than with the intention of seeking to influence or change society. To which end, he 'aims to depict a situation in which we live so forcibly that people on their way home say "We must change that. It can't go on so. We won't be a party to that any more"' (*32*). Weiss's apparent inconsistencies are born perhaps of expediency in part as well as of his undoubted uncertainties. Well might he stress his political ignorance, as he moves from Sade's self-defeating individualism, as he sees it, to Marat's socialism that heralds the future (successful) socialist revolution. Little wonder that Weiss's conflicting viewpoints on *Marat/Sade* between 1963 and 1966 fill some thirty pages in the *Materialienbuch* (*14*).

Weiss's own ambiguity of reaction is matched in the variety of response by the critics to Weiss's play based on differing literary and political emphases. The very titles of a handful of critical pieces that appeared in the sixties, for instance, provide an adequate and telling pointer: '*Marat/Sade* and the Theatre of Unrealism';[20] 'Die Verfolgung und geistige Ermordung des Peter Weiss unter Anleitung des Herrn Kuba';[21] 'Engagement im Historischen';[22] 'Goethe gegen Weiss' (*17*); 'Marat/Sade/Artaud' (*41*); 'History and Cruelty in Peter Weiss's *Marat/Sade*' (*45*).

It is worth mentioning that Weiss's problems with Peter Brook were to continue. The latter was responsible for the subsequent film version of *Marat/Sade* and Weiss was not happy with its progress. We read the following entry in the *Notizbuch* for 17 May 1966 (*7*, pp.498f.): 'Ich bin betrogen, vom Produzenten, von den Agenten u ihren Zuträgern — Brook wird meinem weiteren Weg nicht folgen.'

---

[19]*New York Times*, 26 December 1965.
[20]*Times Literary Supplement*, 17 September 1964.
[21]Eberhard Olias, *Deutsche Fragen*, 1965, p.130.
[22]Ernst Schumacher, *Theater der Zeit*, 1965, Heft 16, p.4.

Weiss's theatrical commitment has never been less than total — from writing the script for a play to being present in the theatre at rehearsals and collaborating with the director, from playing the role of drummer for some performances of his play *Der Turm* to being responsible for the setting of Swinarski's production of *Marat/Sade* (just as Gunilla Palmstierna-Weiss was responsible for the costumes in that same play, and was to become involved in many of Weiss's works) to being writer *and* director of his revised version of Kafka's *Der Prozeß* in Stockholm in 1982 shortly before his death. Understandably total commitment in the quest for total art is in evidence here in *Marat/Sade*.

Epilogue

A fitting tribute to the memory of Peter Weiss was paid by Marcel Reich-Ranicki in the *Frankfurter Allgemeine Zeitung* (12 May 1982), but in fact a very pertinent and fair assessment of Weiss's work had already been provided by that same critic in *Die Zeit*:

> Wir verdanken ihm schließlich das 'Marat'-Drama und einige hervorragende Prosabücher, die zwischen 1960 und 1963 erschienen sind. Und was immer Peter Weiss noch schreiben mag, er kann nur sich selber kompromittieren, nicht sein früheres Werk, das aus der Geschichte der deutschen Literatur nach 1945 nicht mehr wegzudenken ist.[23]

His view is one essentially shared by George Steiner some five years later:

> Nothing in Weiss's productions over the past decade and a half...shows the great gifts of *Marat/Sade* or of those shadowy, perfectly evocative sketches and stories based on his actual childhood and Swedish exile.[24]

Marat/Sade should ultimately be seen in the context of the following revealing entry in Weiss's *Notizbuch*:

> die Partei war für mich ein Kampfinstrument gewesen. Das feste, organisierte Kollektiv stellte das Gegen-

---

[23]January 1970, No.5, p.12.
[24]*Times Literary Supplement*, 2 April 1976, p.402.

gewicht dar zu meinem persönlichen Schwanken u
Zweifeln. Ich wollte in der Partei die Vernunft, die
Folgerichtigkeit verwirklicht sehn, keinen Spielraum
durfte es in ihr geben für Irrationales. Aber es waren
Unklarheiten in der Partei aufgekommen, die meinem
Verlangen nach absoluter Integrität widersprachen. Mein
Zögern war zurückzuführen auf meine Vorbehalte
gegenüber dem Doktrinären u Orthodoxen, ich verlangte
nach offener Kritik. Ich würde meine Skepsis, meine
Unruhe nicht leugnen können — (*8*, p.437)

Weiss came to regard his self-appointed task as that of trying to
reach what George Steiner describes as 'a concordance between the
arts and the state of the common man' (*TLS, idem*), or what Heinrich
Vormweg sees as being 'ein existentiell konkretisierender
permanenter Dialog mit dem Weltgeist in diesem Jahrhundert...eine
individuelle Verwirklichung der geistig-politischen Hauptfragen der
Epoche.'[25] The dialectics of culture and politics are central to an
understanding of *Marat/Sade*, but also of those subsequent plays
Trotzki im Exil and *Hölderlin* (and equally so of his novel *Die
Ästhetik des Widerstands*). That art should serve the Revolution was
undoubtedly Weiss's ideal. His writings reflect, however, only too
clearly the problems involved.

Marat was to give his name to one of the first battleships of the
Soviet navy. It seems appropriate then that Weiss should turn from
the French Revolution of *Marat/Sade* to the Russian Revolution of
Trotzki im Exil, where the respective attitudes of Lenin and the
Dadaists mirror the problem. The latter proclaim a revolution in art
that is based on an anarchic nihilism, whilst Lenin demands a
proletarian culture. When a united front was realized to be
unworkable, some like André Breton turned to support Trotsky, who
for his part had envisaged 'die klassenlose Kunst' and expressed his
views in his work *Literature and Revolution* (1923). Breton, the
voice of doubt in Marxism, went to Trotsky in Mexico and together

---

[25]'Peter Weiss' in *Kritisches Lexikon zur deutschsprachigen
Gegenwartsliteratur*, ed. H.L. Arnold, Munich, 1978ff., p.2.

in 1938 they founded 'La Federacion de l'Art Revolutionaire Independent'. But Trotsky's way was to remain a 'Wunschtraum' (rather as Weiss's own novel *Die Ästhetik des Widerstands* was to remain a 'Wunschautobiographie'). Trotsky is in exile, an exile that is both physical and of the mind; he is sitting at his desk (rather like Marat in his bath), surrounded by his books and papers (denoting therefore the writer as well as the revolutionary), shortly before his own assassination.

With *Hölderlin* we return to the familiar historical framework of the French Revolution. Indeed the play opens with a time-setting of July 1793, and Marat's assassination by Corday is announced at the end of Scene 1. There is no doubt that the rejection politically of *Trotzki im Exil* by Russia and East Germany as being 'patently anti-Soviet in character' jolted Weiss severely and probably contributed to a situation in *Hölderlin* where the two alternative ways of approaching the matter of revolution are presented in a way more directly reminiscent of *Marat/Sade* itself, although the two aspects are now incorporated in the one figure of Hölderlin, as against being represented earlier in two, namely Sade and Marat. The familiar names and situations of the French Revolution are back again, and there is even something of the earlier style in evidence too in the play. Hölderlin's madness is seen as being induced by the collapse of the Revolution in France and in Scene 7 we find him as a patient in a straitjacket in the clinic at Tübingen before finishing up in his tower of isolation, his Charenton, to which he has retreated from the madness of the world of capitalist rulers and thinkers in Germany. Successful revolution was to remain only a dream. A mythical utopian vision of revolution was contained in an extract from his drama *Der Tod des Empedokles* that was inserted at the start of Act 2 as a play within a play (though here too contemporary overtones of Che Guevara are contained). But Sade and Hölderlin are ultimately writers who are defeated by the gap existing for them between ideas and action, theory and practice. The dualism between art and politics is here reflected in the young Marx and Hölderlin who meet in Scene 8:

MARX

    Zwei Wege sind gangbar

    zur Vorbereitung

    grundlegender Veränderung

    Der eine Weg ist

    die Analyse der konkreten

    historischen Situation

    Der andere Weg ist

    die visionäre Formung

    tiefster persönlicher Erfahrung

HÖLDERLIN

    Jedoch

    aber

MARX

    Vor Ihnen

    stell ich die beiden Wege

    als gleichwertig hin

    Daß Sie

    ein halbes Jahrhundert zuvor

    die Umwälzung nicht

    als wissenschaftlich begründete

    Notwendigkeit sondern

    als mythologische Ahnung

    beschrieben

    ist Ihr Fehler nicht

                  (6, p.174)

The thread of continuity is self-evident.

    As for *Marat/Sade* itself, the play's seminal importance in the development of the post-war theatre has continued to be recognized in the regular stagings of the piece over the years world-wide. And, as with other plays by Weiss, *Marat/Sade* too has had its share of newspaper headlines through political controversy. Referring to the possible performance of the play in South Africa, Weiss makes the following entry in his *Notizbuch*:

> Zustimmung für Aufführung Marat im Market Theatre von Barney Simon in Johannesburg, Südafrika. Lehne sonst alle Aufführungen meiner Stücke in diesem Land ab. Dieses Theater mir als progressiv empfohlen. Meine Bedingung: Aufführung nur für 'absolutely non segregated audiences'. Meine Tantiemen sollen den Familien der Opfer von Soweto zur Verfügung gestellt, und dies im Programmheft mitgeteilt werden. Garant: Nadine Gordimer. (*8*, pp.505f.)

His political convictions had in fact meant the stopping of the opening of *Marat/Sade* in Johannesburg in 1969, when he felt he could not permit its showing before segregated audiences in a nation where he believed people were denied human rights. The play incidentally was performed in the March of 1974 at the Black Arts Festival in Soweto. The *Black Review* at the time described the play as depicting 'the replacement of one type of dictatorship by another ruling class which still continued to trample upon people' (presumably with reference to the then emergent Bantu homeland leadership).[26] One of the most recent productions of the play was a performance by students of the University of Exeter as part of the 1989 students' German Drama Festival presented by Lancaster University to coincide with the 40th anniversay of the founding of the Federal Republic of Germany. Weiss would surely not have been amused at this 'souveräne Ironie'!

The undeniable fact remains, however, that the palywright brilliantly achieved in *Marat/Sade* a radical fusion of a number of tendencies to be found in the theatre of the 1960s. He consciously availed himself of Artaud's legacy — the Theatre of Cruelty and its ritual; at the same time, in using the theatre as a metaphor for a play of existential emptiness, Weiss reminds us of the aims of the Theatre of the Absurd. We have also referred earlier to Weiss's admiration

---

[26]*Theatre Quarterly*, 1977-78, Winter, Vol. VII, No.28, 57-62.

for Expressionist drama, and this influence is mirrored in his own use of the theatre here as a utopian, visionary transcendence of the given world. And in his concern to make a commentary on historically verifiable personages and events, Weiss admits into his play the documentary features of the Theatre of Fact. He has succeeded in drawing eloquently on all these possibilities and therein can be detected a basis for much of the resonance of *Marat/Sade*. Its sheer centrality to these several literary or theatrical modes and thematic concerns of modern European theatre mark Weiss's signal success.

Select Bibliography

A. PRIMARY LITERATURE

1. *Die Verfolgung und Ermordung Jean Paul Marats dargestellt durch die Schauspielgruppe des Hospizes zu Charenton unter Anleitung des Herrn de Sade*, fifth version (Frankfurt: Suhrkamp, 1965).
2. *Marat/Sade*, in *Spectaculum*, 35 (Frankfurt: Suhrkamp, 1982), pp.231-304.
3. *The Persecution and Assassination of Marat as Performed by the Inmates of the Asylum of Charenton under the Direction of the Marquis de Sade*, English version by Geoffrey Skelton, verse adaptation by Adrian Mitchell (London: Calder & Boyars, 1965).
4. *Dramen* I und II (Frankfurt: Suhrkamp, 1968).
5. *Fluchtpunkt* (Frankfurt: Suhrkamp, 1962).
6. *Hölderlin* (Frankfurt: Suhrkamp, 1971).
7. *Notizbücher 1960-1971*, I und II (Frankfurt: Suhrkamp, 1982).
8. *Notizbücher 1971-1980*, I und II (Frankfurt: Suhrkamp, 1981).
9. *Stücke* I, II/i und II/ii (Frankfurt: Suhrkamp, 1976/77).
10. *Trotzki im Exil* (Frankfurt: Suhrkamp, 1970).

B. SECONDARY LITERATURE

11. Heinz Ludwig Arnold (ed.), *Peter Weiss. Text + Kritik*, 37 (München: Ed. Text + Kritik, 2nd ed., 1982).
12. Hans-Joachim Bernhard, 'Marat auf der Bühne', *Neue deutsche Literatur* 1965/9, 169-82.
13. Otto F. Best, *Peter Weiss* (Bern: Francke, 1971).
14. Karlheinz Braun (ed.), *Materialien zu Weiss' 'Marat/Sade'* (Frankfurt: Suhrkamp, 1967).
15. Wolfram Buddecke und Helmut Fuhrmann, *Das deutschsprachige Drama seit 1945* (München: Winkler, 1981), pp.380-92.
16. Volker Canaris (ed.), *Über Peter Weiss* (Frankfurt: Suhrkamp, 1970).
17. Wilhelm Emrich, 'Goethe gegen Peter Weiss', in *Die Welt der Literatur*, 9 July 1964.

18. Rainer Gerlach (ed.), *Peter Weiss* (Frankfurt: Suhrkamp, 1984).

19. Wilhelm Girnus, 'Gespräch mit Peter Weiss', *Sinn und Form* XVII (1965), 678-88.

20. John Gross, '1793 and all that', *Encounter*, November 1964, 58-60.

21. Manfred Haiduk, *Der Dramatiker Peter Weiss* (Berlin: Henschel, 1970; 2nd edition 1977).

22. ——. 'Peter Weiss' Drama "Die Verfolgung und Ermordung Jean Paul Marats..."', *Weimarer Beiträge* 12/1 (1966), 81-104, and 12/2 (1966), 186-209.

23. Ian Hilton, *Peter Weiss. A Search for Affinities* (London: Oswald Wolff, 1970).

24. T. Hocke, *Artaud und Weiss. Untersuchung zur theoretischen Konzeption des 'Theaters der Grausamkeit' und ihrer praktischen Wirksamkeit in Peter Weiss' 'Marat/Sade'* (Bern: Lang, 1978).

25. Marianne Kesting, 'Verbrechen, Wahnsinn und Revolte. Peter Weiss' 'Marat/Sade'-Stück und der französische Surrealismus', in *Geschichte als Schauspiel*, ed. W. Hinck (Frankfurt: Suhrkamp, 1981).

26. Ladislaus Löb, 'Peter Weiss's *Marat/Sade*. A portrait of the artist in bourgeois society', *Modern Language Review* 76 (1981), 383-95.

27. Franz Norbert Mennemeier, *Modernes deutsches Drama*, Bd II (München: Fink, 1975), pp.192-246.

28. John Mitfull, 'From Kafka to Brecht: Peter Weiss's development towards Marxism', *German Life and Letters* XX (1966-67), 61-71.

29. Werner Mittenzwei, 'Zwischen Resignation und Auflehnung', *Sinn und Form* XVI (1964), 894-908.

30. Hans-Bernhard Moeller, 'Weiss's reasoning in the madhouse', *Symposium* 20 (1966/2), 163-73.

31. Ulrike Paul, *Vom Geschichtsdrama zur politischen Diskussion* (München: Fink, 1974), pp.111-72.

32. 'Peter Weiss in conversation with A. Alvarez', *Encore*, No.56 (July/August 1965), 19-23.

33. *Peter Weiss — Maleri — Collage — Teckning* (Södertälje: Konsthall, 1976).

34. 'Peter Weiss, Marat and the Marquis de Sade', *The Times* (11 May 1964), p.6.

35. Heinz Plavius, 'Peter Weiss, Marat und die soziale Revolution — ein Grenzfall des Nonkonformismus', *Neue deutsche Literatur* 1965/9, 159-68.

36. 'Playwright of many interests', *The Times* (19 August 1964), p.5.

37. Hans Werner Richter, *Im Etablissement der Schmetterlinge* (München: Hanser, 1986), pp.259-79.

38. Henning Rischbieter, *Peter Weiss* (Velber: Friedrich, 1967).

39. David Roberts, *'Marat/Sade*, or the birth of post-modernism from the spirit of the avantgarde', *New German Critique* 38 (Milwaukee, 1986), 112-30.

40. Peter Schneider, 'Über das Marat-Stück von Peter Weiss', *Neue Rundschau* 4 (1964), 664-72.

41. Susan Sontag, 'Marat/Sade/Artaud', *Partisan Review* XXXII (1965), 210-19.

42. Zbigniew Swiatowski, 'Einsamkeit und Solidarität', *Sinn und Form* XXXV (1983), 126-49.

43. Heinrich Vormweg, *Peter Weiss* (München: Beck, 1981).

44. Ernst Wendt, 'Peter Weiss zwischen den Ideologien', *Akzente* 5 (1965), 415-25.

45. John White, 'History and cruelty in Peter Weiss's *Marat/Sade*, *Modern Language Review* 63 (1968), 437-48.